MOZART

FRANZ NIEMETSCHEK
(from the painting by Romberg in the Collection of Hofrat Dr Ernst
Richter, Vienna)

MOZART

The First Biography

FRANZ NIEMETSCHEK

Translated by
Helen Mautner

with an Introduction by

CLIFF EISEN

Berghahn Books
New York • Oxford

Published in 2007 by

Berghahn Books

www.berghahnbooks.com

©2007 English edition, Berghahn Books

Library of Congress Cataloging-in-Publication Data

Niemetschek, Franz Xaver, 1766-1849.

[Leben des K.K. Kapellmeisters Wolfgang Gottlieb Mozart. English]
Mozart : the first biography / Franz Niemetschek ; translated by
Helen Mautner ; with an introduction by Cliff Eisen. — English ed.
    p. cm.
Includes bibliographical references.
ISBN 1-84545-231-3 (alk. paper)
    1. Mozart, Wolfgang Amadeus, 1756–1791—Biography.
    2. Composers—Austria—Biography. I. Title.

ML410.M9N413 2006
780.92—dc22
[B]   2006019295

British Library Cataloguing in Publication Data

A catalogue record for this book is available from the British Library

Printed in the United States on acid-free paper

ISBN 1-84545-231-3 hardback

INTRODUCTION

CULTURALLY-ENTRENCHED beliefs die hard, no matter the facts. And one of the most enduring music-historical tropes is the legend of Mozart's sorry end: by the time of his death in 1791, the composer was penniless and unappreciated, rejected by the Viennese court, nobility, and public, a mere shell of a man whose only recourse was to escape to a perfect musical world of his own making. At least this is what most biographies tell us. Yet this myth hardly corresponds with the facts. To be sure, Mozart had suffered financial setbacks between 1788 and 1790, although in this respect he was no different from most Viennese musicians: Emperor Joseph II's restrictions on church music, a weak economy, and a war with Turkey all conspired to make life difficult for composers, performers, and music publishers. By 1791, however, Viennese musical life was on the rebound and Mozart, perhaps more than any other local composer, benefitted from this resurgence of musical well-being. In that year alone he was asked to write two operas (*La clemenza di Tito* and *Die Zauberflöte*), at least twelve of his works were published by Viennese music dealers, he had commissions from Hungary and from Amsterdam (to say nothing of the private commission for the Requiem), and he returned to the concert stage with a performance of the concerto K595 on 4 March. When he unexpectedly died, on 5 December, his passing was noted not only in

Viennese newspapers but throughout Europe, even as far away as London: "Died. On the 5th inst. at Vienna, Wolfgang Mozart, the celebrated German composer."[1]

It is a mark of the esteem in which the composer was held that two biographies of Mozart appeared within seven years of his death—musical biography was a rarity at the time. The first, Friedrich Schlichtegroll's 'Johannes Chrysostomos Wolfgang Gottlieb Mozart,' was published at Gotha in 1793.[2] As far as is known, Schlichtegroll never met Mozart and his chief source of information was the composer's sister, Nannerl, who in addition provided Schlichtegroll with reminiscences by the family friend, poet, and Salzburg court trumpeter, Johann Andreas Schachtner. Predictably, the result was a biography that said a great deal about Mozart's childhood—and fixed the idea that, as a family friend, Albert von Mölk, put it: "apart from his music he was almost always a child, and thus he remained"—but not much about the Vienna years from 1781 on.

The second biography of Mozart—and the first wholly independent book on the composer—was Franz Xaver Niemetschek's *Leben des k.k. Kapellmeisters Wolfgang Gottlieb Mozart*, published in Prague, 1798. Born at Sadska in Bohemia on 24 July 1766, Niemetschek studied philosophy at university, earning a doctorate in 1800; shortly afterwards he was appointed professor of philosophy at Prague, where he lectured on logic and ethics. Niemetschek was also one of the earliest music critics in the Bohemian capital and an ardent supporter

---

[1] *The Times*, 24 December 1791, n.p. See Cliff Eisen, *New Mozart Documents* (London, 1991), 154.

[2] In the *Nekrolog auf das Jahr 1791*, 82–112. For an English translation, see Bruce Cooper Clarke, *The annotated Schlichtegroll: Wolfgang Mozart's obituary* (St Anton a.d. Jessnitz, Austria, 1997)

of Italian opera: for him, Mozart represented an aesthetic ideal. It is likely that Niemetschek met Mozart during the latter's visit to Prague in 1791 and he was certainly acquainted not only with Wolfgang's Prague friends but with his widow, Constanze. Apparently their relationship was a close one: after Mozart's death, Niemetschek took over the education of the composer's older son, Carl Thomas (1784–1858).

Although Niemetschek's account of Mozart's early years is taken almost entirely from Schlichtegroll, this represents only a small part of the biography: the bulk of it concerns the Vienna years. Not surprisingly, Niemetschek claimed that Mozart was more appreciated in Prague than anywhere else—one important legacy of his work was the idea that Mozart was neglected in Vienna. And while he tried to sort out fact from fiction, he was sometimes misled, not least by Constanze, who on various occasions provided contradictory information, especially concerning the commissioning, composition, and performance of the Requiem. (At one point Niemetschek claims that no performance of the Requiem "has been traced anywhere"; barely two pages later, however, he notes that Constanze had performed the work for her personal benefit.) Other "facts" are wrong, too. It is not exactly the case, for example, that Mozart's father "gave up all his lessons and occupations, except for his court duties, and devoted himself wholly to [his children's] musical education." On the contrary, Leopold continued to compose works of his own at least until 1770. And the letter by Baron Gottfried van Swieten that Niemetschek cites in connection with Mozart's arrangements of works by Handel is almost certainly a forgery (the letter refers to Mozart's work on *Messiah* but its date, 21 March 1789, falls a good two weeks after the work's performance on

6 March). By the same token, Mozart was not 34 when he died, as Niemetschek twice claims, but 35.

Yet it is not for the "facts" that Niemetschek is still read. Rather it is his biographical and aesthetic appreciation of Mozart that is of lasting significance. And the Mozart that emerges in these pages is almost worthy of sainthood. His nature is gentle and his feelings warm and utterly sincere. He was lost in his art and forgetful of the world when making music. He was kind and generous and upright, honorable, and possessed of a "noble dignity and frankness which so often go with great genius." Mozart was modest and free of pride, conceit, and ingratitude: when the Prague opera orchestra played his works, he "warmly thanked [them] in a letter to Herr Strobach, who was director at the time, and attributed the greater part of the ovation which his music had received in Prague to their excellent rendering."

In short, Niemetschek forges an inseparable bond between Mozart the man and Mozart the artist: ". . . what music-lover during the pure sweet pleasure of listening to Mozart's works of art has not thought with deep emotion of the creator of these delights?" Biography is not about the "facts" of a life but how it is to be understood; art is not separate from biography, but intimately bound up with it. In Mozart's case, biography is a parable of morality as well, albeit morality unrewarded. As a child, Mozart showed his friends and acquaintances "the utter sincerity and warmth of feeling of which his gentle nature was capable. This trait in his character was typical of him when he grew up, and was often his undoing." When he was in Paris in 1778, "his upright nature was not suited to the intrigues and quarrels which in this huge arena of human passions even attempted to strangle the arts." In the end, Mozart is a victim: "if it is really true, as has been definitely asserted—and it is difficult to disbelieve reliable eye-witnesses—that disgruntled singers out of hate, envy and ill-will, tried to spoil [*Le nozze di Figaro*] by continually making mistakes at the first performance, the reader may gather how much the whole coterie of Italian singers and composers feared the superiority of Mozart's genius. . .". Niemetschek's comment on the composer's apparent neglect pretty much sums it up: "the fault certainly did not rest with him."

Nevertheless, there is a redemption of sorts and that is our ability to identify with and emulate Mozart's virtues. This ability, Niemetschek implies, is the mark of a noble spirit; in a passing mention of Haydn (to whom the biography is dedicated) he notes that "real artists are willing to recognize each other's worth!" Ordinary listeners can recognize this too. Or better, anyone who appreciates Mozart's music already shares his virtues since appreciation is otherwise impossible: "above all, his music demands pure feeling and an unspoilt ear. Mozart did not write for those who do not possess these attributes."

CLIFF EISEN

New York, spring 2006

FURTHER READING

H. C. Robbins Landon, *1791: Mozart's Last Year* (London, 1988)

Maynard Solomon, 'The Rochlitz Anecdotes' in *Mozart Studies*, ed. Cliff Eisen (Oxford, 1991), 1–59

William Stafford, *Mozart's Death: A Corrective Survey of the Legends* (London, 1991)

William Stafford, 'The evolution of Mozartian biography' in *The Cambridge Companion to Mozart*, ed. Simon P. Keefe (Cambridge, 2003), 200–214

Mozart family portrait by della Croce (circa 1780)

Leopold Mozart, father (circa 1765)

Anna Maria Mozart, mother (1775)

Nannerl Mozart, sister, Vienna (1762)

Mozart in gala dress, Vienna (1762)

Leopold, Wolfgang, and Nannerl, Paris (1763)

Mozart, Verona (1770)

Archbishop Colloredo (circa 1780)

Joseph II (1780s)

Constanze Weber Mozart, wife, by Hanson (1802)

Franz Xavier Mozart and Karl Mozart, sons, by Hanson (1798)

Mozart, unfinished portrait by Joseph Lange (circa 1782 or 1783)

Mozart, by Barbara Krafft (copy circa 1819 of portrait circa 1780)

This little memorial to immortal Mozart
is dedicated by the author
with deepest homage to
Joseph Haydn
(Kapellmeister to Duke Esterhazy)
Father of the noble art of music
and the favourite of the Muses

The *numbered* footnotes are those of the author himself. Those to which an *asterisk* is affixed have now
been added by way of correction or clarification.

LIFE OF MOZART

As THE SWEET enchantment of Mozart's harmony and the overwhelming stream of his feeling never fail to raise his listeners to ecstatic heights, so the student of human nature cannot but admire the early development and rapid maturity of his creative genius.

From both standpoints Mozart inspires so great an interest that I beg leave to hope that this biographical sketch will prove a not unwelcome offering to the public.

For what music-lover during the pure sweet pleasure of listening to Mozart's works of art has not thought with deep emotion of the creator of these delights? Who has not admired this mighty prince of harmony? For these sensitive people I write this story of his life. May the reader derive as much pleasure from it, as I have done in writing it. At the same time I am performing a duty which gives me a pleasure similar to that which I enjoyed from his works, and the honour of contributing something to the glorification of his name.

The father of our musical Raphael, Leopold Mozart, was the son of a bookbinder in Augsburg who studied in Salzburg and entered the ducal orchestra in 1743. His talent combined with his upright character obtained for him the post of second conductor in 1762. He married Anne Bertlinn* and both were of such prepossessing appearance that, it is said, they were considered the best-looking couple in Salzburg.

Leopold Mozart busied himself with his Court duties; the rest of his time he spent in composing and giving violin instruction. What expert knowledge of this instrument he must have had is proved by his well-known 'Violinschule' published in 1766** and re-issued in 1770.

He was father of seven children, but only two survived—a girl and a boy. The son who was born on 27 January 1756 was called Wolfgang Gottlieb (Amadeus), his sister, who was older, Maria Anna.

As the father soon noticed outstanding musical talent in both his children, he gave up all his lessons and occupations, except for his Court duties, and devoted himself wholly to their musical education.

The unusually high standard of perfection which Mozart's genius attained must be ascribed to this excellent training. Nature herself can achieve much —but neglected or forced into other channels, she loses something of her original strength. The first train of thought and early impressions are of the utmost importance in a child's development. If we now consider Mozart's natural talent set in such fortunate surroundings, we should not be amazed at his precocious comments and performances, and will the more readily believe the facts which I am about to relate. The first impressions which his ear received were of harmony and song; music was the

---

*Usually spelt Pertl.
**In fact 1756.

first word and idea which he comprehended. Thus the heavenly spark of genius which the Almighty had laid in the breast of this dedicated youth must early have been fanned into flame. The comprehensive knowledge of his scholarly father was always available to the awakening genius; so he grew up and so he matured earlier than he could have done if he had been left to his natural development only.

Mozart was just three years old when his sister (then aged seven), had her first clavier lessons, and here the boy's genius first came to light. He would often sit at the clavier of his own accord and amuse himself for hours harmonising in thirds, and when he found them he would play them and was greatly delighted. So his father began to teach him easy pieces; and he saw with delight and astonishment that his pupil exceeded.all human expectations; he generally learnt in half an hour a minuet or a little song and then played it with the correct expression.

Readers will readily understand that little Mozart had a lively temperament and very tender feelings. He entered into his childish playing with a wholeheartedness which made him forget everything else, and love for those around him or for any who occupied themselves with him was his driving force; he asked all with whom he came in contact whether they loved him, and burst into tears if they jokingly denied it.

In fact, even as a child and later as a boy he concentrated entirely on people and things of interest to him, and showed them the utter sincerity and warmth of feeling of which his gentle nature was capable. This trait in his character was typical of him when he grew up, and was often his undoing.

By the time he was six he had made such strides in his music that he started composing little pieces for the clavier which his father then had to write down. From then onwards he was totally absorbed by music, and showed no interest in childish pursuits, unless they were combined with music.

His daily progress was an everlasting wonder to his father, who was continually at his side and could, therefore, watch his every step. And his steps were not those of a clever pupil, but the giant strides of a genius, whose size even his father and teacher could not have foretold, as his development and talent exceeded all possible hopes. The following occurrence, which Schlichtegroll also narrates in his obituary, and which has been confirmed by many other people, will serve as proof.

When Wolfgang was about six years old, his father one day came home from his orchestra with a friend; they found the little musician with a pen in his hand. His father asked him what he was doing.

Wolfgang: 'Writing a concerto for the clavier.'

Father: 'Let me see. That will be a fine thing, to be sure!'

Wolfgang: 'I've not finished it yet.'

Whereupon his father took the music from him and found a mess of notes and smudged blots of ink, as the young composer did not yet know how to use a pen properly. He dipped it too far into the ink, making blots on his paper which he proceeded to wipe off with his hand and then continued to write. When, however, his father looked at the composition a little more closely, his attention was caught with agreeable surprise and he was so indescribably touched, that he wept for joy.

'Look at this, my friend', he said laughingly, 'how the whole piece has been composed correctly according to the rules. Only it cannot be performed, as it is too difficult to play.'

Wolfgang: 'That is why it is called a concerto. It must be practised until it is played properly. Look, this is how it goes!'

Then he began to play it, but could hardly manage to show what his idea had been. For he was of the opinion that playing a concerto and working miracles were one and the same thing.

At about this time the boy had advanced so far that his father, without further ado, decided that the rest of the world should also bear witness to his son's extraordinary talent.

———————

The first journey Leopold undertook with him and his sister was in 1762, when they went to Munich. Here Wolfgang played before the Elector, and he and his sister received the greatest applause.

The second journey took place in the autumn of the same year, that is, while he was still six, when they went to Vienna, where the two infant prodigies were introduced at the Imperial Court.

One of the ladies of the court assured me that both children made a very great impression; people could hardly believe their ears and eyes at the performance. Emperor Francis I, that great lover of the arts, was greatly delighted with the little 'magician' (as he was jokingly called). He often chatted with the boy. All the anecdotes mentioned by Schlichtegroll have been confirmed.

Among other things, the Emperor said in fun
that it was not such a great art to be able to play,
if the keyboard could be seen, but if the keys were
covered, what then? This did not upset Mozart in
the least. The keys were covered and he played just
as well as before.

Even that was nothing so extraordinary, if every
finger was used when playing, but if he were to
play with a single finger that really would be clever.

Still the boy was not put out—he straightway
attempted it, and to everyone's astonishment,
played several pieces quite well in this manner.
Even then he showed a trait of his character which
he was to retain throughout his life—his contempt
for all praise from the nobility and a certain diffi-
dence about playing to them, if they were not, at the
same time, knowledgeable people. When compelled
to do so nevertheless, he would play nothing but
trivial pieces, dances, etc.—unimportant trifles. But
when experts were present he was all fire and enthusiasm.

This characteristic he retained till the end, as we
ourselves observed on his three visits to Prague.

That is exactly what occurred in the presence of
Emperor Francis. As Mozart was seating himself
at the clavier while the Emperor stood at his side,
the young boy said, 'Isn't Herr Wagenseil here?
He understands.' Wagenseil came in, and the child
prodigy said to him, 'I am going to play a concerto
of yours. You must turn the pages for me.'

Perhaps the following anecdote will also add
something to this picture of him.

Of all the Archduchesses, the future Queen Marie
Antoinette of France took most interest in him, and

he had a particular affection for her. When on one occasion he entered the rooms of the late and revered Empress Maria Theresa and was being led around by the little Princes and Princesses, he had the misfortune to slip and fall on the highly polished floor, to which he was not accustomed. Nobody was more eager to help him up than young Antoinette. This touched his little heart so much, that he went straight up to the Empress and praised the great kindness of the little Princess. Who could not love such a child?

The exemplary way in which he handled the clavier, and his knowledge of the art, which he had acquired at an age when most children would not as yet have shown any particular artistic inclination, was admirable enough: surely nothing further could be expected. But this marvellous musical talent, which had been implanted in him by his Creator, knew no bounds, and when once it had been awakened, far outstripped any formal instruction. What one wanted to teach him, he already seemed to know. He had only to turn it over in his mind!

His lessons served merely as an encouragement and as a help to his general development.

Mozart before this played no other instrument but the clavier, although he knew how to play the fiddle before his father realized it, or had given him any kind of violin instruction. I would like to narrate the following incident, which brought this to light, in Schlichtegroll's own words. "Mozart had brought a little violin back from Vienna which had been given him there. Soon after the family returned to Salzburg, Wenzl, who was a violinist himself and was just beginning to compose, came to father Mozart

B

and asked for his opinion about six trios which he had composed in the family's absence. Schachtner, who was still Court trumpeter in Salzburg, and of whom little Mozart was particularly fond, happened to be present. 'The father' (so narrates this reliable witness) 'played the bass on the viola, Wenzl the first violin, and I was supposed to play the second violin. Little Wolfgang begged to be allowed to play the second violin, but his father refused his childish plea, as he had not had any proper instruction yet, and could therefore not possibly perform properly. The child replied that it was not necessary to have had lessons to be able to play the second violin, but his father rather half-heartedly told him to go away and leave him alone. The little boy began to cry bitterly and ran away with his little fiddle. I begged that he should be allowed to play with me. In the end his father agreed and said to him: "All right, then, go and fiddle with Mr Schachtner, but play quietly so that you can't be heard." We began to play and little Mozart fiddled away by my side, but I soon noticed that I was quite superfluous. I laid my fiddle down and looked across at his father, whose eyes were filled with tears which rolled down his cheeks. He was so moved by this scene. Wolfgang in fact played all the six trios. After he had finished, our applause emboldened him to assert that he could also play the first violin. So, to humour him, we made a start and could not help smiling when he likewise managed to play this instrument. And although he played with a certain amount of incorrect and irregular fingering, he never once broke down.'

With what wonderful accuracy he could judge

the finest distinction of tone, how unbelievably reliable his memory was, may be proved by the following occurrence which took place about this time:

Schachtner, as already mentioned, was a friend of the Mozarts and little Mozart's favourite, owned a violin which was very dear to him on account of its soft tone and which he called his 'butter fiddle'. One day he played it. Several days later Schachtner came again and found Wolfgang improvising on his own little fiddle. 'How is your butter fiddle?' asked Wolfgang, and went on improvising. After a short pause he seemed to remember something and said: 'If only you would keep your fiddle at the same pitch! Last time I played it, it was a quarter of a tone lower than mine here.' We laughed at this bold assertion; even the greatest expert would scarcely be able to detect the difference.

His father, however, who had often before been surprised by his son's extraordinary ear for pitch, considered it worth while to put his assertion to the test. The fiddle was fetched and, to everybody's astonishment, his statement was proved to be mathematically correct.

With all his accomplishments and his extraordinary talent, little Mozart was perhaps too industrious for his delicate body. He had to be called away from the clavier, sometimes almost chased away, otherwise he might still have been there at daybreak.

This self-forgetfulness, when he was making music, lasted all his life; he would sit at the clavier every day till late at night—a sure sign of the genius by which he was absorbed, to the almost total exclusion of all else.

One must not, however, believe that he was
incapable of doing anything else. He learnt easily,
entered into everything with great keenness and
enthusiasm, due to his very sensitive nature. He
would cover chairs, tables and floors with numbers
when he was learning arithmetic, and thought and
spoke of nothing but arithmetical problems; he
became in the course of time an adept at figures.

At the same time he was so obedient to and docile
with his parents that he never had to be punished,
and he would neither accept nor eat food without
his father's permission.

As soon as people heard of his talent, he was called
upon to show off his prowess to strangers for whole
days at a time; but he never minded when his
father called him back to the piano. He was always
very kind and friendly with his playmates and was
attached to them with all the affection of his warm
nature—even in his childish amusements, his keenness on music was shown, and games with music
were always his favourites.

When he was seven, in 1763, Mozart and his sister
were taken by their father on their first big music
tour in Germany. The fame of the young genius was
thus spread abroad. He showed his talent and
accomplishment particularly in Munich, where he
not only played a violin concerto before the Elector,
but also played improvisations of his own. They
then went on to Augsburg, Mannheim, Mayence,
Frankfurt, Coblenz, Cologne, Aix-la-Chapelle and
Brussels.

From there they left for France, where the
family stayed for twenty-one weeks. At Versailles
the little eight-year-old boy played the organ in the

Royal Chapel before the King. At that time he was more highly esteemed as an organist than as a clavier-player.

In Paris they gave two subscription concerts for the public, following which an engraving was made of Leopold Mozart and his two children, and people competed in expressions of admiration. It was in Paris, too, that Mozart's first compositions were printed and published. He dedicated his first work to Madame Victoire, the second to the King's daughters and another to Countess Tesse. They are all piano sonatas.

Leaving Paris, the family arrived in England on 10 April 1764. In the same month the children were heard by the Royal Family; in the following month Mozart was asked to play the King's organ. Later they gave a public benefit concert and another in aid of the Foundling Hospital—in both cases the symphonies were by the son. Then they gave one more concert before the King and the nobility. The unusual applause and approval shown by the public everywhere, on hearing this talented boy, were a spur and encouragement to him to perfect himself still more. He also sang arias with great feeling and it must have been touching to see this young pair of prodigies playing on two claviers, or to hear them singing together. The son had progressed so far in his art, that he could play the most difficult master-pieces straight away at sight. In Paris and London, pieces by Handel and Bach were placed before him, which to the astonishment of all experts he was immediately able to perform with accuracy and with proper expression.

When he played before the King of England he

was given, in some instances, merely the bass, to which he promptly played a charming melody.

During this stay in England he wrote six piano sonatas, which were engraved in London, and which he dedicated to the King.

The family spent the summer* of 1765 in Flanders, Brabant and Holland. During a dangerous illness (smallpox) which kept both children in bed for some months, the boy started on another six piano sonatas, and when, on his recovery, he finished them, he had them engraved and dedicated to Princess von Nassau-Weilburg. During his illness his creative energy persisted, and as he was not allowed to leave his bed, he asked to have a board laid over his couch, on which he could write; even while his little fingers were still covered with spots it was difficult to prevent him from writing and playing. This story comes from a very reliable source.

Early in 1766, for the celebration of the coming-of-age of the Prince of Orange, young Mozart composed several symphonies, variations and arias.

After he had played several times for the Heir Apparent, the family travelled to France again, and stayed some time in Paris, and then went on to Swabia *via* Lyons and Switzerland, and lived for a while at Donaueschingen with Prince von Fuerstenburg. At the end of 1766 they returned to Salzburg after an absence of three years.

Here the Mozart family now remained quietly for more than a year. This time of relaxation Mozart employed in a concentrated study of composition, whose greatest depths he had soon fathomed.

*They left England on 1 August.

Emmanuel Bach, Hasse and Handel were his heroes; their works were his permanent study. He did not neglect the old Italian Masters either, whose superiority in regard to melody and profundity in the art of composition compares so favourably with modern Italian composers. Gradually he came ever nearer perfection in his art, in which the world was to recognise the rarity of his achievement.

In the following year, 1768, Mozart went to Vienna and played for the Emperor Joseph, who commanded the twelve-year-old boy to write an opera buffa. It was called *La Finta Semplice*, and was praised by the composer Hasse, and also by Metastasio, but was not performed.

During his stay in Vienna he was often in the company of the poet Metastasio (who was very fond of him), and also of Hasse and Prince Kaunitz; here Mozart was often given an Italian aria at random, which he immediately set to music fully orchestrated, in the presence of everybody. This fact is confirmed by several dependable people still living, from whose own lips I have heard it.

At the consecration of the Chapel of the Orphanage, which was being celebrated at this time, the twelve-year-old Mozart composed the sacred music, and conducted the performance in the presence of members of the Imperial Court.

He spent the year 1769 with his father in Salzburg, devoting some time to mastering the Italian language and the rest to his music studies. In the same year he was appointed Konzertmeister at the Salzburg Court.

Mozart had by now visited all the most important countries of Europe; the fame of his musical talent, which had developed so early, had already spread from the banks of the Danube to the Seine and the Thames; but he had not yet been to the spiritual home of music. Italy's admiration and astonishment had yet to put her seal of fame on him, for at that time it was still considered the Fatherland of music. Similarly, in his striving for perfection, it was of the utmost importance that he should hear singing, the very flower of music, on its native soil, and make the acquaintance of many important people who were then still upholding Italy's musical fame, and that he should learn from them.

In December of the same year, Mozart, therefore, left Salzburg in his father's company. Their first halt was at Innsbruck, where he played a concerto at sight for the Duke Kuenigl with the greatest ease. From there they went to Milan.

In France and England his great talent and exceptional dexterity had evoked admiration. But it was in Italy that he was received and acclaimed with the greatest enthusiasm. Even their national pride and prejudice and chauvinism were swept aside by the shining genius of this boy of twelve. He seemed to them an apparition from heaven, a lord of music!

His genius was so much esteemed that after several public proofs of his talent in Milan he was given a written contract for the series of operas for the coming Carnival of 1771. From there he travelled in March 1770 to Bologna—a town which was second only to Naples for its great musical reputation.

Here the young artist found an enthusiastic

admirer in the famous musician Padre Martini[1],
the celebrated master of counterpoint and a well-
known musical author in Italy. Real artists are
willing to recognise each other's worth!

Italians have shown, not only in the case of
Mozart, but also in regard to our own compatriot
Misliweczek that they are willing to recognise talent
even if shown by people of other nationalities.
What great respect was paid to this famous Bo-
hemian in Naples and Rome!

Padre Martini was filled with admiration, as were
also other musicians present, when Mozart was
given the theme of a fugue and, after inventing
suitable variations and elaborations, immediately
sat down and played the complete fugue.

On hearing him at Florence, people considered
that his genius had been underrated, when he
played for Marquis de Ligniville, who was himself
an eminent master of counterpoint. He played
variations on any theme given him, and read at
sight anything that was laid before him with such
ease that one would have thought he had written
it himself. And the truth of the statement that there
is an understanding between all choice spirits who
recognise their kinship was shown, when in Florence
Mozart made the acquaintance of young Thomas
Linley from England, who was only fourteen. He
was a pupil of the famous violinist Nardini, although
himself already a virtuoso and master of the instrument. They soon became intimate friends; it was
not merely a boyish friendship but was the tender-

[1]Without my reminding them, readers will realise that this
Martini is not to be confused with the present opera
composer, who wrote *Cosa Rara*.

ness of two kindred souls; they respected one another as artists and behaved like adults. How sad was the day of parting! On their last day together Linley brought Mozart a poem which had been specially composed by the poetess Corilla. Tearfully they embraced, and Linley, with expressions of pain and grief, accompanied the carriage as far as the gate.

From Florence, father and son travelled to Rome, arriving there in Easter week. Here Mozart had ample opportunity of hearing many masterpieces of noble church music, performed at this solemn season in celebration of the world's Redemption. In the forefront was the famous *Miserere*, which was sung by the choir in the Sistine Chapel on the Wednesday and Friday of that week. This is considered to be a supreme example of noble and sublime choral singing and the *non plus ultra* of musical art; so much so that, according to the story narrated in the Nekrolog, papal musicians were forbidden to make a copy of it under penalty of excommunication.

This gave Mozart the idea of listening attentively and then of writing it down from memory when he reached home. It was an unexpected success; he took the manuscript with him again on the Friday when there was another performance, so that he could make any corrections or fill in any omissions.

Soon word of his achievement spread through Rome, occasioning great excitement and admiration, particularly when he sang it at a concert in the presence of Christophori, the castrato singer who had sung it in the Chapel. Mozart's triumph was

completed by Christophori's praise. Anyone aware
of the great art required for this complex choral
music for so many voices will certainly be amazed
at this achievement. What musical memory and
what knowledge of composition he must have had to
be capable, not only of understanding, but at the
same time of memorising such a work! To be able
to do so must have entailed greater powers than are
found in the majority of artists.

In Naples, where he went after leaving Rome, he
found as many admirers as in the other two Italian
towns, for every impartial listener felt obliged to
pay homage to his genius. Mozart, as a man,
plucked with all his power at the heartstrings of
every sensitive person; what must his Italian
audiences have thought when they saw before them
merely a boy, but heard a mature artist? They took
him for a magician, which Mozart undoubtedly
was, but his magic did not lie in his ring, as was
suggested in Naples (for when he took it off, at the
request of the audience, his playing was no less
enchanting than it had been before). We can
hardly realise the astonishment and admiration
displayed. From Naples, Mozart returned to Rome
at the special request of one by whom artists are
rarely invited. It was the Pope himself, who, having
heard of this wonderful boy, wanted to see the young
musician in person. He was presented, received a
medal, and was invested with the Order of the
Golden Spur.

On his return from Rome to Milan, he again
made a short stay at Bologna where he was unani-
mously elected member and 'maestro' of the 'Accademia filarmonica'. As a test he had to write a four-

part fugue suitable for church performance. He was, therefore, locked in a room on his own. He took only half-an-hour and duly obtained his Diploma.

In all these towns he received offers of opera contracts for the coming Carnival; as he had already promised one for Milan he had to refuse. So he hurried on, and his opera entitled *Mitridate* appeared at the end of 1770 on 26 December. It received general applause and there were twenty consecutive performances. On the strength of this, he immediately received a written contract for the opera seria for the Carnival of 1773. It was called *Lucio Silla* and met with even greater approval, for it was performed twenty-six times without a break.

On his journey back from Italy in 1771 he visited Venice and Verona; here he was presented with a diploma as a member of the Philharmonic Society.[2] He arrived back in Salzburg after an absence in Italy of more than fifteen months. The rewards of this long journey were valuable knowledge, new ideas, a more refined taste, and the admiration of a nation which seemed called upon by its very nature to be arbiter of taste in matters of music.

On his arrival in Salzburg Mozart found a letter from Count Firmian of Milan in which, on behalf of Empress Maria Theresa, he requested Mozart to write a big dramatic serenata[3] for the wedding of Archduke Ferdinand. For this celebration Hasse, who was the oldest musician, wrote the opera, and Mozart, who was the youngest, wrote the serenata.

2All these decorations, as well as the Papal Cross, have been kept by his widow in his memory.
3Serenatas were a kind of cantata, with a dramatic theme as basis. They were, in fact, similar to the conventional oratorios, whose content was, however, religious.

The Empress seemed so to have arranged it delib-
erately. This serenata bore the title *Ascanio in Alba*.
During the celebrations, the opera and serenata
were performed alternately. When the new Archbishop of Salzburg was elected in 1772, Mozart also
wrote a dramatic serenata entitled *Lo sogno di
Scipione*.

Journeys which Mozart undertook in the years
1773 and 1774 to Vienna and Munich were the
occasions for the writing of several musical masterpieces; he also wrote the comic opera *La finta
Giardiniera* and several Masses for the Royal
Orchestra at Munich at this period.

In the year 1775 Mozart wrote the operetta *Il Re
Pastore*, which was very well received and belongs
to those of his earlier works which are still appreciated
even now; for in these the great genius, which
prevails throughout his later works, was becoming
manifest.

This particular point (that is, when he was
twenty) may be taken as the beginning of the epoch
of his perfection as a master, for, from then onwards,
he always shone in a brilliant light and with effort-
less superiority; all the works that he composed since
then have become classics, and have won for him
the crown of immortality. But we must continue
with the story of his life, and will criticise the best of
his works of this period in a separate section.

Mozart's fame had now been established. Every
large city, where he had demonstrated his talent,
received him with joy and listened to his works with

delight. The expectations of the public were more than justified by his dual talents as pianist and composer.

Among all the towns, Paris was no doubt the most agreeable to him as an artist; the more so as his art had already been recognised there by an enthusiastic audience. But he himself had no taste for French music. Moreover, his upright nature was not suited to the intrigues and quarrels which in this huge arena of human passions even attempted to strangle the arts. He therefore came back from Paris in 1777 whither he had journeyed for the last time with his mother, but he returned alone, as she had died there. With his sensitive feelings this loss must have added to the discomfort of his stay in Paris. At the end of 1778 he was back again in Salzburg.

The Bavarian Court, which had so often been witness of his artistic talent, and in particular the Elector, that great patron of the fine arts, was very fond of Mozart's music. He therefore received a contract to write an opera seria for the Carnival to be held in Munich in 1781.

For this purpose Mozart wrote the noble work *Idomeneo*. The youthful vigour displayed by the composer had paved the way for the wealth of sentiment and warmth of feeling which this opera contains.

He counted the time spent in Munich amongst the pleasantest days of his life, and never forgot the cordial friendship which he there enjoyed with so many estimable people.

From Munich he was recalled to Vienna by an order of the Archbishop of Salzburg; and from then onwards, that is, from his twenty-fifth year, he lived in this Imperial City, which was valuable to Mozart not only on account of the public's obvious love of music, but also because of the many eminent composers who had made their home there.

From here his famous compositions spread to Bohemia and then to the rest of Germany and gave music a big impetus in a new direction, to the disadvantage, however, of those who later imitated him.

In Vienna, above all, his piano-playing was admired; for although Vienna had many great masters of this instrument, which had since become everyone's favourite, yet nobody could come up to our Mozart! His admirable dexterity, which particularly in the left hand and the bass were considered quite unique, his feeling and delicacy, and beautiful expression, of which only a Mozart was capable, were the attractions of his playing, which together with his abundant ideas and his knowledge of composition must have enthralled every listener and made Mozart the greatest pianist of his time.

His piano compositions, all kinds of sonatas, variations and concerti soon became well-known and much esteemed. Surprise was evinced, each time a new work appeared, at the originality of his style and his thoughts—everybody was amazed at the heights to which his music soared.

In Vienna too he found the composer who most nearly resembled himself: I speak of the famous creator of *Alceste* and *Iphigenia*—Ritter von Gluck, a Bohemian by birth. His company and the continual study of his noble works afforded Mozart a great deal of sustenance and influenced his operatic compositions. Mozart also became a most sincere admirer of the great and incomparable Joseph

Haydn, who had already become the pride of music,
and now, since Mozart's death, remains our favourite and our delight. Mozart often called him his
teacher.

Soon after Mozart had ended his stay in Vienna,
Emperor Joseph II had the idea, so worthy of a
German Emperor, of suppressing the taste for
Italian opera by supporting German operettas and
singers, and by giving more support to the music of
the Fatherland. He therefore collected together the
best men and women singers and Mozart was to
write the opera. For these performers, then, he
composed the well-known and much-loved operetta
Die Entfuehrung in the year 1782.

It created a great stir; and the cunning Italians
soon realised that such a man might be a menace
to their childish tinkling. Jealousy now reared its
head with typical Italian venom. The monarch,
who at heart was charmed by this deeply stirring
music, said to Mozart nevertheless: 'Too beautiful
for our ears and an extraordinary number of notes,
dear Mozart.' 'Just as many, Your Majesty, as are
necessary', he replied with that noble dignity and
frankness which so often go with great genius. He
realised that this was not a personal opinion, but
just a repetition of somebody else's words.

I must not forget to mention that Mozart at this
time courted and married Constanze Weber, his
still surviving widow, sister of the famous singer
Lange. The influence of the romantic mood on the
composition of this opera is there for all to hear;
for everyone knows it is pervaded with sweet thoughts
and languishing love.

I cannot describe the sensation it made in Vienna

from my own experience—but I was witness to the enthusiasm which it aroused in Prague among knowledgeable and ignorant people alike. It was as if what had hitherto been taken for music was nothing of the kind. Everyone was transported—amazed at the novel harmonies and at the original passages for wind instruments. Now the Bohemians proceeded to seek out his works, and in the same year, Mozart's symphonies and piano music were to be heard at all the best concerts. From now onwards preference for his works was shown by the Bohemians. All the connoisseurs and artists of our capital were Mozart's staunch admirers, the most ardent ambassadors of his fame.[4]

Mozart had lived up till this time, in spite of his great fame, without regular employment, that is, without a fixed income. Piano instruction and subscription concerts given to an intimate circle of the aristocracy were the most regular sources of income, out of which it would have been hard to save anything in a town like Vienna.

At this period he wrote the most beautiful piano sonatas with and without accompaniment, and concerti which are now available to everybody.

In the year 1785 he had six masterly quartets engraved with a dedication to his friend, the musician Joseph Haydn, which is a worthy sign of his esteem for this great man. Not only does the homage of an artist like Mozart enhance Haydn's fame, but it is also to Mozart's credit, and makes us realise the tenderness of his feelings, considering

---

[4]Especially Herren Duschek, Kucharz, Praupner, Johann Kozeluch (not Leopold, who lives in Vienna), Loschek, Maschek and Kunz.

that he himself had such wonderful talent.

Certainly Mozart could not have honoured Haydn with a better work than with these quartets, which contain a mine of precious thoughts and which are, indeed, models of composition.

In the eyes of the connoisseur this work is of importance equal to any of his operatic compositions. Everything in it has been carefully thought out and perfected. One can see he that has taken the trouble to deserve Haydn's praise.

The French comedy *Figaro*, by Beaumarchais, was being acted at all the theatres at about this time and it was to change his whole fortune. Mozart turned it into an opera on the instructions of Emperor Joseph, and through the addition of music made it famous in the Italian Opera Theatre. It was performed in Vienna by the Italian Opera Company. If it is really true, as has been definitely asserted— and it is difficult to disbelieve reliable eye-witnesses —that disgruntled singers out of hate, envy and ill-will, tried to spoil the opera by continually making mistakes at the first performance, the reader may gather how much the whole coterie of Italian singers and composers feared the superiority of Mozart's genius and how right I was a short while ago in my remarks about *Die Entfuehrung*. They slandered him and did their best to belittle his art. How Mozart's art had to fight for its very existence, until it triumphed completely!

It is said that the singers had peremptorily to be called to their duty by the late monarch, as Mozart in his dismay had come to the royal box during the first act and had drawn attention to what was happening.

As in Bohemia all his works were recognised and appreciated at their true value; thus it was with the opera, too. It was staged in the year 1787 by the Bondini Company and received such an ovation as was only to be equalled by that given to *The Magic Flute* at a later date. It is the absolute truth when I state that this opera was performed almost without a break throughout the winter and that it greatly alleviated the straitened circumstances of the manager. The enthusiasm shown by the public was without precedent; they could not hear it often enough. A piano version was made by one of our best masters, Herr Kucharz; it was arranged for wind parts, as a quintet and for German dances; in short, Figaro's tunes echoed through the streets and the parks; even the harpist on the alehouse bench had to play 'Non piu andrai' if he wanted to attract any attention at all. This manifestation was admittedly mostly due to the excellence of the work; but only a public which had so much feeling for the beautiful in music and which included so many real connoisseurs could have immediately recognised merit; in addition, there was the incomparable orchestra of our opera, which understood how to execute Mozart's ideas so accurately and diligently. For on these worthy men, who were mostly not professional concert players, but nevertheless very knowledgeable and capable, the new harmony and fire and eloquence of the songs made an immediate and lasting impression. The well-known Orchestra Director Strobach, since deceased, declared that at each performance he and his colleagues were so excited that they would gladly have started from the beginning again in spite of the hard work it entailed. Admir-

ation for the composer of this music went so far that
Count Johann Thun, one of our principal noblemen
and a lover of music, who himself retained a first-
class orchestra, invited Mozart to Prague and offered
him accommodation, expenses, and every comfort
in his own home. Mozart was too thrilled at the impression which his music had made on the Bohemians, too eager to become acquainted with such a
music-loving nation, for him not to seize the opportunity with pleasure. He came to Prague in 1787; on
the day of his arrival *Figaro* was performed and
Mozart appeared in it. At once the news of his presence spread in the stalls, and as soon as the overture
had ended everyone broke into welcoming applause.

In answer to a universal request, he gave a
piano recital at a large concert in the Opera House.
The theatre had never been so full as on this occasion;
never had there been such unanimous enthusiasm
as that awakened by his heavenly playing. We did
not, in fact, know what to admire most, whether
the extraordinary compositions or his extraordinary
playing; together they made such an overwhelming
impression on us that we felt we had been bewitched.
When Mozart had finished the concert he continued
improvising alone on the piano for half-an-hour.
We were beside ourselves with joy and gave vent
to our overwrought feelings in enthusiastic applause.
In reality his improvisations exceeded anything
that can be imagined in the way of piano-playing,
as the highest degree of the composer's art was
combined with perfection of playing. This concert
was quite a unique occasion for the people of Prague.
Mozart likewise counted this day as one of the
happiest of his life.

The symphonies which he composed for this occasion are real masterpieces of instrumental composition, which are played with great élan and fire, so that the very soul is carried to sublime heights. This applies particularly to the symphony in D major, which is still a favourite in Prague, although it has no doubt been heard a hundred times.

The opera director Bondini commissioned Mozart to compose a new opera for the Prague stage for the following winter, which the latter gladly undertook to do, as he had experienced how much the Bohemians appreciated his music and how well they executed it. This he often mentioned to his acquaintances in Prague, where a hero-worshipping responsive public and real friends carried him, so to speak, on their hands. He warmly thanked the opera orchestra in a letter to Herr Strobach, who was director at the time, and attributed the greater part of the ovation which his music had received in Prague to their excellent rendering.[5] This trait in his character, insignificant though it may seem, is very beautiful; it shows that pride, conceit or ingratitude were not faults of his—as is so often the case with lesser virtuosi.

Towards the winter of 1787, thanks to his contract, Mozart again came to Prague, and there finished the crown of his masterpieces, the opera *Il dissoluto punito* or *Don Giovanni*.

The Bohemians are proud that he had recognized and done honour to their good taste in opera, by creating this work with all the power of his genius. '*Don Giovanni* was written for Prague'—more need

[5]The author has read the letter in the original, and found it very well written.

not be said to prove what great respect Mozart had
paid to the musical perception of the Bohemians.
He succeeded admirably in recognising their taste
and in stirring their feelings; for no opera has been
popular for so long at the Theatre as *Don Giovanni*.
It is now ten years since it was first performed—
and it is still being heard with pleasure and still
attracts a large audience. In short, *Don Giovanni* is
the favourite opera of the élite of Prague. When
Mozart appeared at the piano in the orchestra at the
first performance, everybody in the crowded theatre
applauded by clapping enthusiastically. In fact,
in Prague, Mozart continually received great and
indubitable proof of respect and admiration, which
were certainly genuine, as neither prejudice nor
fashion but pure feeling for his art was the cause. His
beautiful works were loved and admired; how could
one remain indifferent to the great composer himself?

In the year 1789, in the month of December,
Mozart wrote the Italian opera *Cosi fan tutte* or *The
School for Lovers*; everyone was astonished that this
man could have demeaned himself to waste his
heavenly melodies on such a worthless libretto.
It did not, however, lie in his power to refuse the
commission, and the libretto was specially provided.
In this period he also travelled *via* Leipzig and
Dresden to Berlin.[6] His great reputation went ahead
of him and no one was disappointed in the expectations which had been aroused. The King of Prussia,
that generous patron and lover of music, was quite
taken with him and gave him excellent proof of his
respect. How genuine and lasting this was, is proved
by the royal generosity with which the monarch in

6He undertook this in the spring of the year 1789.

later years befriended and supported Mozart's widow in Berlin.

Mozart was up till now without either post or a regular income. In spite of the fact that his talents were so well known and his compositions sought, no thought was given to rewarding or supporting him. It is true he had often earned considerable sums, but with an insecure and irregular income, added to the frequent accouchements and lengthy illnesses of his wife in an expensive town like Vienna, Mozart in fact very nearly starved. He therefore decided to leave the city, where there was no place for a genius like Mozart. His plan was to go to England, where he might have expected a better fate, as he had often received invitations and attractive offers from that country.

He was on the point of departure when Emperor Joseph conferred on him the title of Imperial Chamber Composer with an annual salary of eight-hundred florins, and the promise that his future would be assured. Mozart swallowed his pride, accepted the offer and remained. This contract was made on 7 December 1787.

I leave it to my reader to judge for himself the causes of the long neglect of such a great artist. The fault certainly did not rest with him; one must therefore blame his unworldly nature, for he was incapable of currying favour.

Many people were jealous and hostile, and tried their utmost to belittle his talents by slander; but with unprejudiced folk, who had not been tarred with the brush of fashion, the triumph of his art was supreme. All the most erudite recognised his genius. I will give an example.

Baron van Swieten, who was recognised both as a worthy statesman and man of learning, a true music-lover with much feeling for the oratorios of the great Handel, often had the works of this famous composer performed at private concerts, these being too strong a diet for the more delicate taste of the day. He therefore availed himself of our Mozart's talents, who was able to give new life to Handel's noble ideas by his ardent feeling, and through the magic of his instrumentation to make them enjoyable to our own generation.[7] Baron van Swieten often corresponded on this matter with Mozart and wrote to him on one occasion as follows:

March 21—1789

Your idea of converting the text of the tepid aria into a recitative is excellent, and as I do not know if you still have the words, I am sending you a copy of them. Anybody who can clothe Handel's work with such taste and dignity, that it finds acceptance amongst the fashionable world, and contrives at the same time to show proper respect for the composer's worth, and an understanding of his intentions, has done all that I have wanted. That is how I view your achievements, and now I need no longer speak of confidence, but only of my wish to receive the recitative soon.—SWIETEN.

This excellent man, noble beyond all praise, remained throughout a true friend of Mozart's and is now guardian to the orphans he left.

The Turkish war and the consequent death of the unfortunate monarch, Joseph, robbed Mozart

[7]Mozart worked on Handel's *Acis and Galatea, Messiah, St Cecilia* and *Alexander's Feast* for him in the years 1788-90.

of a great support for his hopes; he still remained Kapellmeister with eight-hundred florins but without a sphere of activity.

But his end, too, was approaching; he was not to outlive the great monarch very long. The year 1791, in which the deaths of so many notable people occurred, was also destined to snatch away the pride of music. Mozart had, however, given generously to posterity out of the richness of his genius. Therefore this year is just as noteworthy for the creation of his beautiful compositions, as it is saddened by his early death. In the same year, in fact very near the end of his life, he wrote the music for *The Magic Flute*, for the opera seria *La Clemenza di Tito*, and the sublime Requiem, which he was unable to finish. These three works alone have assured him of the first rank among composers of his generation, and have obtained for him immortal fame. Sadness at his early death is thus increased by the reflection which is bound to occur to thoughtful people, 'Oh, how much this man might yet have achieved, and what harmonies he might yet have created!'

He set to music *The Magic Flute*, which had been written by the well-known Schickaneder, an old acquaintance of his. The music for the opera *La Clemenza di Tito* had been commissioned by the Bohemian Parliament for the coronation of Emperor Leopold. He began the latter in his travelling coach on the way to Vienna, and he finished it in the short space of eighteen days in Prague.

The story of his last work, the Requiem mentioned above, is as obscure as it is strange.

Shortly before the coronation of Emperor Leopold, even before Mozart had received the order to travel to Prague, a letter without signature was brought him by an unknown messenger, which with many flattering remarks contained an enquiry as to whether he would be willing to undertake to write a Requiem Mass. What would be the cost, and how long would it take to complete?

Mozart, who never made the least move without his wife's knowledge, told her of this remarkable request, and at the same time expressed a wish to try his hand at this type of composition, the more so as the higher forms of church music had always appealed to his genius. She advised him to accept the offer. He therefore replied to his anonymous patron that he would write a Requiem for a given sum; he could not state exactly how long it would take. He, however, wished to know where the work was to be delivered when ready. In a short while the same messenger appeared again, bringing back not only the sum stipulated but also the promise, as Mozart had been so modest in his price, that he would receive another payment on receipt of the composition. He should, moreover, write according to his own ideas and mood, but he should not trouble to find out who had given the order, as it would assuredly be in vain.

In the meantime he received a very flattering and advantageous offer to write the opera seria for the Coronation of Emperor Leopold in Prague. It was too much of a temptation for him to refuse to go to Prague to write for his beloved Bohemians.

Just as Mozart and his wife were getting into the travelling coach, the messenger appeared like a ghost and pulled at her coat. 'What about the

Requiem?' he asked. Mozart excused himself on account of the necessity for the journey, and the impossibility of informing his anonymous patron; in any case it would be the first task on his return, and it was only a question whether the stranger could wait so long. The messenger seemed to be quite satisfied.

While he was in Prague Mozart became ill and was continually receiving medical attention. He was pale and his expression was sad, although his good humour was often shown in merry jest with his friends.

On his return to Vienna he at once started on his Requiem Mass and worked at it with great energy and interest; but his indisposition increased visibly and made him depressed. His wife realised it with misgivings. One day when she was driving in the Prater with him, to give him a little distraction and amusement, and they were sitting by themselves, Mozart began to speak of death, and declared that he was writing the Requiem for himself. Tears came to the eyes of this sensitive man: 'I feel definitely', he continued, 'that I will not last much longer; I am sure I have been poisoned. I cannot rid myself of this idea.'

This speech fell like a load on his wife's heart. She was unable to console him, or to convince him that his melancholy imaginings were without foundation. As she felt that he was on the verge of a serious illness, and that the Requiem was getting on his over-sensitive nerves, she called in the doctor, and took the score of the composition away from him.

His health actually improved somewhat, and he

was able to finish a small cantata, which had been ordered by a Society for a celebration. The splendid way in which it was performed and the applause it received gave his energies a new impetus. He became more cheerful and repeatedly expressed the wish to continue and finish the Requiem. His wife could no longer find an excuse for withholding his music.

This hopeful state of affairs was but short-lived; in a few days he became despondent once more, weaker and more listless, until he sank back in his sick-bed from which, alas, he never rose again.

On the day of his death he asked for the score to be brought to his bedside. 'Did I not say before, that I was writing this Requiem for myself?' After saying this, he looked yet again with tears in his eyes through the whole work. This was the last sad sight he had of his beloved art, which was destined to become immortal.

Soon after his death the messenger arrived and asked for the composition in its incomplete state, and it was given him. From that moment onwards Mozart's widow never saw him again and never found out anything, either about the Requiem or by whom it had been commissioned. The reader can imagine that no trouble was spared in trying to find the mysterious messenger, but all efforts and attempts proved in vain.[8]

[8]His widow possesses the score of this, and treasures it as a precious possession. The author speaks of the event as he has often heard it from the lips of Mozart's widow, and leaves it to the reader to draw his own conclusions. He has seen one of the notes which the 'unknown' patron wrote to Mozart. Nothing much can be gathered from it as it is very short. Mozart is requested to send the Requiem, and to state a sum for which he would compose a certain number of quartets each year. Why did the unknown 'Admirer of

Mozart remained completely conscious during his illness right to the end and died calmly, although regretfully. This can be readily understood, when one considers that Mozart had been officially appointed to the post of Kapellmeister in the Church of St Stephen with all the emoluments connected therewith since time immemorial, and had the happy prospect of living peacefully without financial worries. He also received, almost simultaneously, commissions from Hungary and Amsterdam, as well as many orders and contracts for works to be delivered at regular intervals.

This extraordinary accumulation of happy auguries for a better future, the sad state of his financial affairs as they actually existed, the sight of his unhappy wife, the thought of his two young children; all these did not make the bitterness of his death any sweeter, particularly as this much admired artist, in his thirty-fifth year,* had never been a stoic: 'Just now', thus he often complained in his illness, 'when I could have gone on living so peacefully, I must depart. I must leave my art now that I am no longer a slave of fashion, am no longer tied to speculators; when I could follow the paths along which my spirit leads me, free and independent to write only when I am inspired. I must leave my family, my poor children, just when I would have been in a better position to look after

Mozart's talents' (thus he chose to call himself) prefer to remain anonymous? What has happened to the Requiem? No performance of the piece has been traced anywhere. Mozart's friends would be only too pleased to find an explanation, for one cannot think of any plausible reason for such mysterious concealment.

*In fact he was in his thirty-sixth year.

their welfare.' His death followed in the night of 5 December 1791. The doctors did not agree on the cause of his death. Countless tears were shed for Mozart, not only in Vienna, but possibly even more in Prague, where he was so much loved and admired. Every connoisseur, every music-lover felt that he was irreplaceable; and in truth up till now there has been no cause to alter this melancholy opinion. It seemed impossible that a man who had produced such great works, who had given us such pure joy, should be no more.

In Vienna his funeral was conducted with due solemnity; Prague, too, showed her heartfelt sympathy; genuine sorrow for our favourite was universally felt. The worthy music director Joseph Strobach, a friend of the deceased,[9] celebrated Mass for Mozart in his church of St Niklas on 14 December of the same year. No more moving and noble memorial service could be recalled. A choir of one hundred and twenty persons, chosen from the foremost artists of Prague, who had all, with touching eagerness, offered their services, sang the masterly Requiem of our famous compatriot Rosetti (actually Roesler), under the direction of noble Strobach, with such intense pathos that it must have made a deep impression on the assembled congregation. More than three thousand people, both the nobility and ordinary citizens (as many as the church could hold), had assembled—all deeply moved and saddened at the early death of this artist, now gone for ever.

Somewhat later, on 28 December 1791, a band

---

[9]He was honoured both as artist and man, and died in December 1794.

of staunch admirers undertook to organise a public concert in the National Theatre for the benefit of his orphans and widow, and some of the best but lesser known of Mozart's works were performed. This very worthy memorial to the dead was supported by the people of Prague to their utmost capacity, in particular because, by so doing, they took the opportunity of showing their appreciation of Mozart's genius by liberally helping to support his helpless orphans. The theatre was full and the takings considerable. How happy is an artist whose talents win him such friends![10]

In Vienna his widow was treated with equal generosity. Mozart bequeathed to his family nothing but the fame of his name. Their means of support depended on the generosity of a grateful people to whom Mozart had given so many hours of delight, and to whom he had afforded so much pleasure through his inexhaustible talent. And we can truly say that they in their turn tried to repay their debt of gratitude. His widow had the strangely commissioned Requiem Mass performed for her benefit. The great reputation of this masterpiece, and the desire to help his orphans, drew a large public, and we must give credit to the patrons of art in Vienna, and recognise that even after six years they have not become indifferent to Mozart's name!

At all the concerts held annually for his widow's benefit the house is full, and the takings good. At

[10]For fear of offending the extreme modesty of these friends of Mozart, I do not venture to mention their names, though it is only with difficulty that I resist the urge to do so. Prague knows them, in any case, for other notable virtues of theirs. The author pays his tribute to their noble-mindedness.

some of these concerts the music of *Clemenza di Tito*
was also performed with great success, and the
Viennese public still listen with pleasure.

But the generosity of the late Emperor Leopold,
that benign monarch, who was such a friend of the
arts and sciences, but unfortunately died so young,
exceeded everything which had hitherto been done
for Mozart's widow.

Mozart's enemies and slanderers became so
vehement, particularly towards the end of his life
and after his death, that some of the rumours even
reached the emperor's ears.

These stories and lies were so shameless, so
scandalous, that the monarch, not being informed
to the contrary, was quite indignant. In addition to
disgraceful inventions and exaggerations of excesses
which they said Mozart had committed, it was
maintained that he had left debts to the value of no
less than thirty thousand florins—at which the
monarch was absolutely astounded.

The widow had just decided to ask the monarch
for a pension. A noble-minded woman, who had
been an excellent pupil of Mozart's, informed her
how her husband's name was being slandered at
court, and advised her, when she obtained an
audience, to tell the benevolent emperor the real
facts.

The widow soon had an opportunity of following
this advice:

'Your Majesty, everybody has enemies', she said
with feeling at the audience, 'but nobody has been
more strenuously and continuously attacked and
slandered by his enemies than my husband, merely
because he had such great talent! People have had

the audacity to tell your Majesty many lies about him: the debts he left behind him have been exaggerated tenfold. I vouch with my life that three thousand florins would liquidate all his debts. And these debts have not been rashly incurred. We have had no fixed income; we have had many children, and I suffered a serious and costly illness lasting a year and a half. Your Majesty, can you not make allowances, you with your kind heart?'

'If it really is as you say', said the monarch, 'then there is still time to do something for you. Let a concert be given of the works he left, and I will support it.'

He kindly acceded to her petition, and in a short while she was allowed a pension of 260 florins, which in itself was little enough, but as Mozart had only been employed for three years, and his widow was really ineligible for a pension at all, it must be regarded as a gracious act. The concert was given, the immortal monarch fulfilled his generous promise, and the widow was thereby enabled to pay off her husband's debts.

From this occurrence one can gather how many of the malicious stories about the confusion of his financial affairs, his extravagance and such-like defamation of character, could have been true. As it was impossible to belittle his greatness as an artist, ill-natured people tried to defame his moral character; the common practice of small-minded people, to whom all merit and greatness are obnoxious, particularly when they threaten to spoil their own meagre reputations.

A desire to be fair to a man of such merit demands

D

that we try to wipe out such blemishes from the portraits of the great. If the same fairness is shown to Mozart, as one would wish shown to oneself, even then he could not serve as a model of economy and thrift. It is true, he should have been more careful with his money; but is a genius not allowed any weaknesses or failings? Lay your hand on your heart, you who are so critical of him, and say with Horace:

'*Quid tu? Nullane habes vitia?*'

And are you, in any of the arts, a Mozart? The excuse for the debts which he left we have just heard from his widow; and her reasons are certainly not unfounded.

Of all his children only two sons survived him, of whom the younger was only four months old when his father died. He is called Wolfgang and shows great talent for music. It would indeed be strange if his father's assertion, made in jest, were realised, that the boy would become a second Mozart, because he once cried on the same note as Mozart had just been playing. But the son lacks the tender hand of a father, which had guided Mozart's genius in his own formative years.

In north Germany Mozart's fame spread after the performance of *The Magic Flute*. It was from that time (after his death) that his other work began to attract notice there. Thus Mozart never lived to see the extraordinary effect which his works of art produced—this blossoming of his fame. But his widow reaped the harvest of this noble enthusiasm on the journey which she undertook through north Germany in 1796. She realised everywhere to her infinite delight how readily Germans recognise and respect true merit and how deeply Mozart's songs impressed them. She is moved when she thinks of her stay in Leipzig, Halle, Hamburg and Berlin.

On her visit to Berlin in February 1796 His Majesty the late King William II, that great music-lover, and the whole Court, gave ample proof of love and respect for Mozart's genius. She obtained written permission to use the Royal Theatre and orchestra for a concert in recognition of her husband's talent. The undertaking was not only supported generously by the king, but by the people themselves. It is impossible to describe the great and moving effect produced on the king and the unusually large audience by the songs from the opera *La Clemenza di Tito*. All were enthusiastic, the well-known singers, the first-class orchestra and the public. 'The immortal artist's spirit' (this is how a weekly Berlin journal, in which the concert is very interestingly described, expresses it) 'seemed to hover over the assembly when at the beginning of the overture to *The Magic Flute*, so ably performed by the orchestra, a solemn, almost religious hush pervaded the audience.' The written permit,[11] wherein the King of Prussia gives such real proof of his good taste and his respect for German talent, reads as follows:

'His Royal Majesty, the King of Prussia, etc.,

[11]Everybody who knows Mozart's works will be gratified at this enthusiasm; for he will gather from it that the Berlin public had a truer feeling for the beauties of the music than the critics. At least, the unfavourable criticism of this opera in the January number (1796) of the monthly journal 'Teutschland' was evidently reversed. It is said that it was written by Kapellmeister Reichardt, but it is unbelievable to the author that Reichardt could have written anything so biassed and childish.

gives himself the very great pleasure of proving,
in compliance with the request of Mozart's
widow, how much His Majesty admires the
talent of her deceased husband and regrets the
unfortunate circumstances which prevented him
from gathering the fruits of his labour. His
Majesty, therefore, grants Mozart's widow permission to use the Grand Opera House and its
own Orchestra for the performance of *La
Clemenza di Tito* and has accordingly given the
necessary instructions to the Baron von der
Reck, to whom she should refer, and with whom
she should arrange the date and any other
relevant details.'

Berlin, 14 February, 1796.   Fr. William

That is what the king thought of Mozart's
talent. The graciousness of his act naturally had
great value; but the charming way in which it was
demonstrated increases its worth considerably. The
widow never speaks without tears of sheer gratitude
about the graciousness of the king, and boasts of the
many friendly people she met in Berlin.

There was nothing special about the physique of
this extraordinary man; he was small and his coun-
tenance, except for his large intense eyes, gave no
signs of his genius. His glance was unsteady and
absent-minded, except when he was seated at the
piano; then his whole face changed. A concentrated
and serious look would come into his eyes; at every
movement of his muscles the expression of what he

was playing could be observed, and this awakened similar feelings in the listener.

He had small, beautiful hands; he moved them so gracefully and naturally across the keyboard that eyes and ears were equally enchanted. It is astonishing that his hands had such a wide stretch, particularly in the bass. This achievement he himself ascribed to his assiduous study of Bach's works.

The ungainliness of his appearance, his small build, was due to the overtaxing of his brain in his youth and the lack of exercise in his childhood. He was, however, born of good-looking parents and is himself said to have been a beautiful child; but from the age of six he was permanently in a sitting posture, and he was also beginning to write at that time, too. And how much this man wrote, particularly in his latter years! It is well-known that Mozart preferred to play and compose at night, and as his work was often urgent it can be imagined how so delicate a physique as his must have been impaired. These were probably the chief causes of his untimely death (if, in fact, it was not hastened unnaturally).

But in this ungainly exterior dwelt a spirit of such stature as nature but seldom bestows even on her most favoured ones.

The greatness and extent of his genius may be judged by his early and exceptionally rapid development, and by the heights of perfection he achieved in his art. Never had a musician covered the whole wide realm of his art, and succeeded in every field, as Mozart did. From the creation of an opera to a simple song; from the grandeur of a symphony to a dainty dance, his works always bear the stamp of rich imagination, of delicate feelings, of exquisite taste. They have a novelty and originality which are a true sign of genius. Even that which is considered a failing in him only proves his strength and independence in wishing to tread new paths. Just consider the ease with which he created most of his works, and the perfection he simultaneously attained in piano-playing!

All these rare and varied attributes, so closely woven together, determine the rank which is his due among the leading artists. He was indisputably one of the foremost creative men of genius who, with their art, bring an age to a close, and at the same time open fresh paths and give new ideas to their successors. After their appearance, art generally remains static or recedes.

Among the fine arts, none is so much a slave to fashion and modern taste as music. As music merely serves as entertainment and is only really appreciated by the individual, and as there is no meeting place or institution through which public taste could be rightly directed, as, moreover music theory is too vague and has been developed too little even to guide artists themselves or to present them with an ideal, music always sways backwards and forwards between the mood of the moment, the prejudices of a pampered taste, and the standard set by great artists, and is never able to attain perfection.

Furthermore, her signs and manifestations are so uncertain, and the ear, by means of which she communicates with the spirit, is so unreliable a messenger; its sensations are too obscure for us to decide with any degree of certainty where true beauty lies. Whatever pleases the masses is considered beautiful. Anything new has a strong

attraction and is in consequence sure of victory over
the old; so that old music and old fashions are
synonymous. For very few people have enough
feeling for art, or enough knowledge to differentiate
between real beauty and tawdriness. While those
with finer sensibility are more than usually moved by
masterpieces, the street musicians are still churning
out *Die zwei Schwestern von Prag* and the *Tyroler
Wastel* and such-like pretty trifles for so long that the
echo of more beautiful music vanishes. Subsequently
we only learn the names of the masters from books;
the sound of their heavenly harmonies is no longer
heard. That is mostly the sad fate of music. What
strength, what classical content must have been
found in Mozart's works if the effect he made
is an exception to this generalisation? The true
beauty of his music is best appreciated when it has
been heard several times, or studied seriously. Have
we ever tired of *Figaro, Don Giovanni* or *Titus*
throughout the many years they have been performed? Do we not enjoy listening to his piano
concertos, sonatas and songs as much the thirtieth
as the first time? Who has plumbed the depths of
beauty of his violin quartets and quintets even after
hearing them many times? This is the real touch-
stone of classical worth! The masterpieces of Rome
and Greece are appreciated the more often they are
read and the maturer our taste becomes. This
applies equally to knowledgeable as well as ignorant
people when listening to Mozart's music, particularly
to his dramatic works. Those were our feelings at
the first performance of *Don Giovanni* and especially
La Clemenza di Tito.

In addition to the quality and superiority of

Mozart's style just mentioned, the attentive appraiser of his works will notice how he tries, with his fine perception, accurately to interpret each character, with due regard to environment and emotions, *reddere convenientia cuique*. This characteristic showed the real vocation he possessed for dramatic composition and is at the same time an explanation of his magic, and of the great effect of his works. In consequence, each composition has a very distinct character of its own, which is even shown by the choice of key. People who know his works will not require any specific examples of this, as all the operas composed by him have this characteristic to a high degree. This is best exemplified in the whole of *La Clemenza di Tito*. How different are ordinary compositions! There the songs are of so indeterminate a character that they would do equally well for a Mass or an opera buffa.

Another distinguishing characteristic of his works is the way in which great composition is combined with tenderness and grace. This unity is only possible in artists of Mozart's stature. Experience gives us proof of this—how seldom do we come upon compositions which are satisfactory in both respects! Either they are merely contrapuntal works of art, which adhere to all the rules of harmony, but the composer is unable to add warmth, grace and charm which are the magical means of producing emotion; or they are merely dull, lifeless little songs, lacking both sense and coherence, hardly capable, with their sugary tinkling, of giving even fleeting pleasure.

How different it is when we consider Mozart! In his work what is known as the art of composition fuses so well with charm, grace and melody that one seems made for the other and all are of equal importance in attaining the desired effect. And yet how sparing he was in the use of 'sugar and spice'. He recognised the higher demands of art and nature. He wrote what his genius dictated, what his good taste considered fitting, irrespective of whether or not it was to the liking of the stalls. In this way, he formed his own public, convinced that real beauty like truth will in the end be recognised and appreciated. Great artists who have had the courage to go their own way, and have not pandered to prevailing fashion, have always acted likewise.

The main feature of his beautiful and graceful orchestration is the novel way in which he employs wind instruments. They had never previously been used with such artistic effect. Here his genius is shown to be without precedent or rival.

He judged with extreme accuracy the nature and range of all instruments, plotted new paths for them and from each of them obtained the utmost effect, so that the greatest melodic potentiality was realised. This has evoked the admiration of all experts, and will always remain a pattern and guide for the discerning.

How gently the sound of his wind instruments caresses the main theme! How aptly they then blend with the voice! What delicate turns! What virtuosity and variety throughout! Then again when the object or effect demands, how striking is the contrast! What a mighty upsurge of passion! Even in non-vocal pieces, Mozart taught his instruments to sing with such feeling that the listener scarcely realises the absence of the human voice.

With his constant use of wind instruments Mozart yet understood perfectly well how to prevent over-loading, how to judge the exact time and place to make his effect. Never is an instrument wasted or misused and, therefore, redundant. But he alone knew how to achieve his most magical effects with true economy, entailing the least effort, often through a single note on an instrument, by means of a chord or a trumpet blast. How far beneath him are many of his imitators.

However great, however original, Mozart may be in his instrumental work, his mightiest achievement is revealed in his settings of songs for the human voice. Here he earned for himself two-fold recognition—both outstanding. His good taste led him back to mother nature and to simple genuine feelings. He dared to defy the Italian singers[12] and to forbid all unnecessary embellishments, orna-mentations and trills. For that reason all his songs are simple, natural, forceful, a pure expression of feeling and of the character and environment of the individual concerned. The meaning of the text is always so conveyed, that one feels like exclaiming:

[12]This is also the reason for the distaste of singers for his works. An even more compelling reason is their unwillingness—ignorant as they were—to take the trouble to study his songs. Mozart, however, did occasionally make an exception. But was he always free to do what he liked when the work had been commissioned? Did he not have to be friendly towards the singers, if he did not wish them to spoil his songs? Also for the sake of the impresario, it was necessary to have regard to the prejudices of the stalls. The two arias of the 'Queen of the Night' in *The Magic Flute* he wrote specially to suit the voice of his sister-in-law Hoffer. That is why one would need to know something of the singers for whom he wrote, in order to be able to form a correct opinion about his dramatic works.

'Truly the music itself seems to speak'. But Mozart seems to surpass himself when he composes music for several voices, trios, quartets, quintets, etc., i.e. for choruses. He is excellent in his truly unique opera finales. What riches! What an infinite number of variations and elaborations! How the voices blend! How beautifully they unite to form a charming whole, bringing forth new harmonies. And yet each is only expressing its own particular feeling. Often the greatest variety and the strongest individuality are here united. We may find beautiful arias by other composers, but nobody can compare with Mozart when it comes to choral work.

But who can unravel all the countless felicities, the fathomless beauties of his art? Who can describe in words his new, original, sublime, and sonorous music? Listen with an open mind, and you will feel this more keenly than can be expressed in words. That is why it never fails to have effect, when it is performed with accuracy and enthusiasm. It is certainly not easy to follow his flights of imagination, and as he has worked out each note to harmonise, there is not such enormous disparity even when the uncouth hands of alehouse fiddlers dare to touch his sublime works.

The most eminent musicians recognised the greatness of his genius and admired his works. Joseph Haydn, the favourite of the Muses, who even in old age still has a youthful spirit, is certainly a supremely competent and dependable judge.

His opinion is unprejudiced because he is recognised as a trustworthy man, and Mozart's fame might rival his own. As early as 1785, when Mozart's father was still alive, Haydn said to him when they

met in Vienna, 'I swear before God and as an honest
man that I consider your son the greatest composer
of whom I have ever heard; he has taste and
possesses a thorough knowledge of the art of
composition.'

In December of the year 1787 this great man
wrote the following remarkable letter to a friend in
Prague, with whom he had been in continual
correspondence and who was asking Haydn to write
a comic opera for Prague:

'You ask me for an opera buffa; with pleasure
if you merely wish to possess some songs composed by me for yourself. But I cannot be of
service to you if you want them to be performed
on the stage at Prague, as all my operas are much
too dependent on our own cast (Esterhaz in
Hungary), and in fact would never be a success,
as they are intended for this particular locality. It
would be quite a different matter to have the
invaluable opportunity of composing an entirely
new work for your Theatre. Even then it would
need courage to run the great risk of putting
myself in competition with such a man as
Mozart.

'For if I were to make as lasting an impression
on music lovers, particularly the eminent ones,
as Mozart's inimitable works have done, nations
would compete to possess such a treasure within
their boundaries. Prague must hold on to this
precious man—but he must also have recom-
pense, for without that, the story of men of
great talent is sad indeed, and gives those who
come after, little encouragement to make further
efforts. For lack of this, unfortunately, so many

who began in hope have succumbed. I am simply furious that this unique Mozart has not yet been engaged by an Imperial or Royal Court.

'Pardon my wandering from the subject—Mozart is a man very dear to me.

I remain, etc.

JOSEPH HAYDN.

P.S. Please convey my compliments to the Prague Orchestra and the virtuosi there.'[13]

If that is Haydn's opinion and if the great man himself speaks so enthusiastically—a Haydn who alone among musicians might easily have been consoled for his loss—what sense is there in the outcry of a few lesser men who wish to compete with him?

Herr H. Naumann, music director of the Elector of Saxony, showed his esteem and admiration for Mozart quite recently. He was on a visit to Prague and spoke touchingly on the subject to Mozart's son, to whom he was introduced by his friend Miss D[uschek]. Whoever knows the modest and unassuming manner of this famous man will certainly not doubt the sincerity of what he said.[14]

---

[13]I have to thank a noble-hearted friend of Herr Roth of Prague, to whom the letter was written, for this precious document, and I take this opportunity formally to acknowledge my indebtedness to this noble friend of Haydn's, and music-lover of fine taste. The letter is one of the most beautiful flowers strewn on the grave of the artist who died all too young—and an embellishment to this biographical sketch. Because it reveals so much of the heart and soul of the writer, as well as of Mozart himself, I have had it printed from the original, and hope to have made a welcome present to the many friends of this grand old man, particularly here in Prague.

[14]The author had the privilege of being an eye-witness of this beautiful scene.

How much Gluck treasured him has already been mentioned.

The large body of good musicians in Prague rightly deserve a prominent place among the judges of Mozart's great talent. Most of them speak with respect of Mozart's works, which is a noteworthy proof of their knowledge and their open-heartedness.

Some have been mentioned previously. Worthy Mr D[uschek] and his wife, who as an artiste and as a cultured woman received acclaim and public esteem, were among Mozart's most treasured friends and admirers. How many excellent artists, of whom Bohemia can boast—how many talented amateurs of good taste, who in any other country would count as virtuosi, would I have to mention if I were to enumerate all his friends and admirers in Bohemia?

But in order to get to know Mozart completely as a musician, we should watch him at his desk when he is composing his immortal works.

Mozart wrote everything with so much ease and speed that at first sight it might be mistaken for superficiality and haste; he never touched the piano while writing. He could see the completed work clearly and vividly when it came to him. His great theoretical knowledge gave him an insight into the whole harmony. We rarely find anything corrected or altered in his concerto scores. This does not mean that he just wrote down anything that came into his head. In his mind the work was already complete before he sat down at his desk. When he received the libretto for a vocal composition, he went about for some time, concentrating on it until his imagination was fired. Then he proceeded to work out his ideas at the piano; and only then did he sit down and write. That is why he found the writing itself so easy. While at work on it he would often joke and chatter. It has already been mentioned that even in manhood he spent half the night at the piano. It was then that he created his loveliest songs. In the peaceful hours of the night, when there was nothing to distract his thoughts, his imagination came alive and unfolded a whole wealth of sound, which nature had implanted in his mind. Then Mozart was filled with sentiment and well-being—most beautiful harmonies seemed to flow from his very fingers. Only those who have heard him at such moments can really appreciate the depth and, in fact, the full extent of his genius: free and indifferent to anything else, his spirit soared aloft to the very highest regions of his art. In such moments of poetic mood, Mozart laid up inexhaustible stores. On these stores he was able subsequently to draw for use in his immortal works.

Moreover, everyone will realise that a rich vein of thought was required. Without this his art would have remained sterile. There are, of course, composers who through painstaking industry manage to bring forth a few ideas, but how soon the source runs dry! But in succeeding works we hear nothing but repetition, and writing to the same formula.

We have already noticed that even while he was still a boy Mozart composed with ease: evidence that it derived from genius. In his later years he continued to surprise people similarly, even those who were well aware of his talent. The overture to *Don Giovanni* is a remarkable example of this.

Mozart wrote this opera in October 1787 in Prague. It was quite complete, had been rehearsed and was to be performed two days later; only the overture was still lacking.

His friends were in a great state of agitation, which increased every hour, but this seemed merely to amuse him; the more embarrassed they became, the more light-hearted Mozart appeared. At last, on the evening before the day of the first performance, when he had been frivolous long enough, he went into his room towards midnight, began writing, and in a few hours had completed this admirable masterpiece, which connoisseurs rank even higher than the overture to *The Magic Flute*. The copyists were only just ready in time for the performance, and the opera orchestra, whose skill Mozart well knew, played it excellently 'prima vista'.[15]

The music for *The Magic Flute* was already finished in July 1791. In the middle of August, Mozart went to Prague, and there he wrote *La Clemenza di Tito* in eighteen days, and it was produced on 5 September. In the middle of the month he returned to Vienna, and a few days before the performance (on 30 September) of *The Magic Flute* he wrote a masterly overture for it, and the Priests' March at the beginning of the second act.

Such examples could be multiplied many times. His exceptional memory had already been evident in his youth; the *Miserere* memorised in Rome gives ample proof of this. He retained it right till the end.

As his works were in unbelievable demand, he was never quite sure whether a new work of his,

15This occurrence is common knowledge in Prague.

even while it was being copied, had not been stolen. So he generally wrote only a line for one hand in his piano concertos, and played the rest from memory. It is said that he once played from memory a piano concerto which he had not looked at for a considerable time, as he left the principal part at home in his hurry.

His hearing was so acute, he recognised the subtleties of sound so precisely and correctly, that he noticed the least mistake or discord, even in the loudest orchestra, and could tell exactly which instrument was in error. Nothing annoyed him more than restlessness, fuss or chatter while music was being played. Then this quiet, friendly man would become extremely annoyed, and showed it in no uncertain way. It is well-known that once in the middle of playing he got up, though with reluctance, and left the inattentive audience. Many people were greatly offended at this; but it was they who were in the wrong. Everything he played he felt very intensely himself—his whole sensitive being was wrapped up in it. How could he then tolerate insensitiveness and inattention, or how could disturbing chatter keep him in the right temper and frame of mind? As a dedicated artist he became oblivious of all external considerations.

We can judge what fine sensibility he had, and how keen his artistic feeling was, when we hear that he was wont to be moved to tears during the performance of good music; particularly when listening to something composed by the two great Haydns. But it was not only music, but any affecting event which gripped and stirred his whole being. His imagination was always active, always occupied

E

with music; that is the reason why he often appeared absent-minded and forgetful.

Mozart was so great an artist! Nobody who has studied human nature will be surprised to learn that this man, who was such a perfect artist, was not such a perfect man in his ordinary dealings. Music was his chief and favourite interest in life—and his whole thoughts and feelings were centred on it; all the powers he had acquired were directed to this one end. Is it surprising if he devoted too little attention to other matters? He was a complete artist, and to an admirable degree—that should be enough. Who can draw the line of his genius so exactly as to declare that Mozart had no talent or ability for anything but his music? Admittedly, we tend more and more to consider artistic genius to be a lower or aesthetic attribute of the soul, but we are, nevertheless, aware that music generally entails great insight into, and judgment and knowledge of, affairs in general. This supposition is all the more certain in the case of Mozart, as he was no ordinary virtuoso of one instrument alone, but covered the whole wide field of music with all possible strength and skill.

Indeed, how beautiful and enviable are the effects that a musician produces! With sweet harmony he delights thousands of sensitive people; he creates pure bliss for them; he elevates, softens, consoles! Even after his death he lives on in his echoing songs—thousands bless and admire him.

Mozart had, while still a youth, shown great aptitude for acquiring the knowledge which it was found necessary to teach him, and had made rapid progress; we have already mentioned his liking for arithmetic. When he was older he still enjoyed it, and was a particularly good arithmetician. He was an equally good linguist. He understood French, English, Italian and German. He learnt Latin only in his later years, and then just enough to understand the church texts, which he had to set to music. In all other languages he had read the leading authors and understood them. He often wrote verse himself; mostly only of a humorous kind.[16] In other subjects Mozart had at least as much factual knowledge as was necessary for a cultured man.

It is to be regretted that he never wrote about his art. From a letter to F.v.T.* (one of his girl pupils), about the performance of a piano fantasy specially written for her, we realise that he not only had a thorough knowledge of music from a practical point of view, but also of its theory.

In an issue of a Berlin musical journal a few years ago, it was stated that Mozart, in fact, had no higher education. It is difficult to know what the writer understands by 'higher education'. What does one demand of an artist? Should he also be an author, a journalist, a politician? Mozart had seen the world, he knew the literature of its most civilised countries, had shown everywhere an open and receptive mind; what did he lack of higher culture? No sensible person would assume that, because he had been neither to school nor university, he was uncultured.

Mozart was an upright, man and had a friendly

[16]This was the case, among others, at the death of a much-loved starling, which he had given a proper gravestone in his hired garden, and on which he had written an inscription. He was very fond of animals, and—particularly—birds.
*Frau von Trattnern.

disposition. Natural benevolence and rare feelings of good-will and friendship were his characteristics. He succumbed to these generous inclinations, and was often deceived because of his instinctive trust of others. In fact, he often gave comfort and hospitality to his greatest enemies and slanderers.

Although he was often able to penetrate hidden depths of character with a quick glance, generally speaking he was too good-natured to be a shrewd judge of it. His unusual upbringing, with the irregular mode of life led on his many travels, combined to render him an indifferent judge of the human heart. To this may be attributed many of the imprudent acts in his life.

Moreover, Mozart was always very receptive to the pleasures of entertainment and friendship. Among his friends he was as confiding as a child, full of fun; he showed this by most amusing ideas. His friends in Prague still remember with pleasure the happy hours spent in his company; they cannot praise his guileless nature enough. In his presence we quite forgot that we were in the company of Mozart, the much-admired artist.

He never betrayed that art-pedantry which is so objectionable in many young Apollos. He spoke seldom and little about his art, and always with charming modesty. High esteem for true merit, and regard for the individual, influenced his judgment of works of art. He was always very touched when he spoke of the two Haydns or other great masters. We would not have suspected that we were listening to the almighty Mozart, but rather to one of their enthusiastic pupils.

I must not omit to mention an incident which

shows not only his sense of justice and his dislike of unkind fault-finding, but also his high regard for Joseph Haydn. It may also serve as an example of his ready wit.

At a private party a new work of Joseph Haydn was being performed. Besides Mozart there were a number of other musicians present, among them a certain man who was never known to praise anyone but himself. He was standing next to Mozart and found fault with one thing after another. For a while Mozart listened patiently: when he could bear it no longer and the fault-finder once more conceitedly declared: 'I would not have done that', Mozart retorted: 'Neither would I, but do you know why? Because neither of us could have thought of anything so appropriate.' By this remark he made for himself yet another irreconcilable enemy.

With extreme modesty, Mozart combined a noble consciousness of his dignity as an artist. How could he possibly have been unaware of his greatness? But he never sought the applause of the multitude. Even as a child he was moved only by the praise of a connoisseur. That is why he was quite indifferent to inquisitive people who came merely to stare at him. Sometimes his indifference possibly went too far. Occasionally, even in the presence of people of the highest rank, he could not be persuaded to play; or he would merely play trifles, if he saw that they were neither connoisseurs nor lovers of music. But Mozart was the most obliging man in the world when he saw that one possessed real feeling for his art; then he would often play for hours to someone quite unknown and unimportant. With

encouraging interest he listened to the efforts of
young artists and, by expressing praise, awakened
dormant self-confidence. There were numerous
examples of this during his stay in Prague, and
many a reader will confirm this report from his own
experience.

Dissimulation and flattery were equally foreign to
his innocent nature, and every compulsion in
matters of the spirit was repugnant. Open and
candid in his utterances and replies, he not seldom
offended the *amour-propre* of others and thereby
made many an enemy. Not only did his great art and
work find a way to the most reserved natures and
evoke tenderness, but they also furnished him with
friends who loved him with all their hearts, and who
were very anxious about his welfare. It would hurt
the fine feelings of these noble people were I to
mention them by name. In any case, how could I
name and know them all?

As for this reason I am not permitted to speak of
the generous friendship of B.v.S.* and a particular
merchant B. in Vienna, I may be allowed at least
to mention here the outstanding kindness shown by
one Viennese citizen to Mozart. The good man, a
butcher by trade, without knowing Mozart person-
ally, merely carried away by admiration for his art,
gave Mozart's ailing wife (who, on account of her
lame foot, was ordered by her doctor to have special
baths made of cooked giblets) the opportunity of
undergoing this treatment in greater comfort in his
own home for a considerable time. He not only
supplied her with this offal free of charge, thereby
saving Mozart an outlay of several hundred florins,

*Baron van Swieten.

but did not charge for accommodation in his home during the treatment. Such instances of the enthusiasm for Mozart's genius are manifold.

But Mozart had enemies too, numerous, irreconcilable enemies, who pursued him even after his death. But how could he have lacked these, being such a great artist and such an upright man? And these are the tainted sources from which flowed so many ugly tales of his frivolity and extravagance. Mozart was a man, therefore as liable to human failings as anyone else. The very characteristics and strength which were needed for his great talent were also the origin and cause of many a blunder. They brought out inclinations which are not found in ordinary persons. His upbringing and mode of life until he settled in Vienna were not of a kind to give him knowledge either of human nature or experience of the world. Just imagine such a tender youngster—a musician of his sensitivity—being left alone in a town like Vienna. Is any more required to make one indulgent towards his faults? In fact we must be sceptical about these stories, as the majority are certainly completely untrue, and are nothing but bare-faced lies, manufactured out of jealousy by envious people. We have already discovered this in regard to the debts he left.

It is not difficult to understand why the world so readily believed in these failings of his, when we consider that a musician is generally assumed to be extravagant and wasteful. But many examples of outstanding artists show how seldom this prejudice is in fact justified.

Mozart was happy in his marriage to Constanze Weber. He found in her a good and loving wife, who was able to fall in with his every mood, and thereby win his complete confidence and exercise great influence over him. This, however, she used only in preventing him from making hasty decisions. He loved her dearly, confided everything to her, even his petty sins—and she forgave him with loving-kindness and tenderness. Vienna was witness to this and his widow still thinks nostalgically of the days of her marriage.[17]

His greatest pleasure was music. If his wife wanted to give him a special surprise at a family festivity, she would secretly arrange a performance of a new church composition by Michael or Joseph Haydn.

He was very fond of billiards, probably because it gave him physical exercise. He had a billiard table at home. There he and his wife played every day. In the summer he obtained exquisite pleasure from the beauties of nature, and enjoyed them whenever he could. He rented a small place on the outskirts of Vienna every summer.

He worked at an astonishing pace in his last years. We can see how much he often composed in a single month from the complete catalogue of his compositions from 1784 till his death, in which he entered in his own hand the theme and date of completion of every piece.[18] Only by consideration

[17]This worthy woman conducts herself in a seemly way in her widowhood, and is a good mother to both her children. She lives in Vienna on her pension and a small income from the money her husband left.

[18]The author had the original by him when writing this biography.

of the power and fertility of his genius is it possible
to comprehend how he could have done such an
enormous amount of work. Thus in the last four
months of his life, when he was already ailing and
had been on two journeys, he wrote:—

1. A piano cantata, 'Die ihr des unermesslichen
   Weltalls Schoepfer ehrt.'
2. *The Magic Flute.*
3. *La Clemenza di Tito.*
4. A clarinet concerto for H. Stadler.
5. A freemason's cantata for full choir.
6. The Requiem.

An enormous effort, which exhausted his strength!

Thus Mozart became a wonder in his art, the
favourite of his age. His short but brilliant life as an
artist marks a new epoch in the history of music.

The great and fiery spirit which pervades his
work and the overwhelming feeling he shows over-
power every susceptible heart with irresistible force.
The sweet magic of his harmonies delights the ear;
abundance of ideas and novelty of expression make
listening to his music a lasting pleasure. Whoever
has once found Mozart to his taste will find little
satisfaction in other music. And all this perfection
he reached at an age when ordinary artists would
hardly have completed their education!

When he died, his reputation had attained heights
such as the most fortunate artist can rarely expect
—and how short was his life! He had not yet
reached his thirty-fifth year when he died! What
might his inexhaustible genius have still given to the
world? His was a rare gift of nature; but still more
rare was his high degree of diligence and taste.

Nature gave him much; but he was able to achieve even more!

Had he gone to England, his fame would have shone beside Handel's immortal name. In Germany his genius was often not appreciated, his grave is not even marked with a bad inscription.

At his death several funeral cantatas were written; among them the two by Wesseley and Karl Kannabich, the younger, of Munich, were outstanding.

The commemoration service which the law students in Prague held at the Accademia in the year 1794, dedicated to Mozart's memory, in the presence of his widow, was simple but dignified. It was beautified by a poem written by Herr Meinerth. A few stanzas from it are worthy of quotation here:

He was too early taken from our midst
Who touched the chords of feeling with such
    skill,
And brought their sharpest tones in harmony.
An angry thunder-breathing God has struck
Where flowed before the peaceful meadow
    springs.

And now the hills are growing green again
But even they can not obscure him quite;
From out the bolts and bars of graves one thing
Streams forth, yet ever-young, divine. It is
The high clear spirit which to all eternity
Blossoms and defies the abhorred shears.

And now the strings' vibrations and the songs
Of rapture, and the turmoil of the heart
All help to bring to mind the sleeping life—
Attend! Angelic harmonies ring out
'Tis Mozart! Crowned he is with radiance,
And in your very midst his spirit moves
On fairy footsteps.

Some Notes about his works

THERE is probably no branch of music in which Mozart has not tried his skill with complete success.

He achieved most fame through his dramatic music and piano compositions. If we regard his works, particularly his dramatic ones, in the order of their appearance, we clearly recognise his rapid strides to perfection. A whole torrent of youthful imagination gushes forth and never-ending expressions of tenderness pervade his earlier works, such as the opera *Idomeneo* and *Die Entfuehrung*, and to some extent in *Figaro* as well. There is more warmth than light—the mass of song and harmony is not so distinct, as in his later works, in which this storm of feeling becomes ever gentler; everything becomes lighter, simpler and more correct. Nowhere is this ripening of taste more obvious than in *La Clemenza di Tito*. From this, one can judge what might still justifiably have been expected of Mozart.

In Vienna, his Italian operas were not received with such great applause as in Prague and in other towns of Germany. The reason for this was not due to the public—which had been enchanted by his German operas—but more to the influence of the foreign singers and the state of the Court Theatre. This is all the more credible as *La Clemenza di Tito* was very much appreciated when repeatedly performed at benefit concerts for Mozart's widow, and is still enjoyed. For Italy they are unattainable heights

—as music there is anything but perfect, as is well-known, and there is a striking lack of wind instrument players. In fact, the majority of singers are too ignorant of their art to be able to intone correctly, or to be able to render Mozart's songs properly. Their national prejudices act as a barrier, because the songs are fruits springing from German soil.

His *Figaro*, was, however, performed at a few theatres, but pitifully badly and without the Finale. In Florence, after nine unsuccessful rehearsals, the first act of *Don Giovanni* was considered incapable of performance.[19]

In Paris, his symphonies and airs are now performed at large concerts. Some art critics have, however, with subtle ingenuity recognised the excellence of his instrumentation (the more mechanical side of his art) but have criticised the vocal part, which is merely matter for the soul. They contend that Mozart's writing for the voice was not as great as his instrumentation.

Within the limits of this narrative, there is not space to show the groundlessness of this opinion nor, indeed, to consider Mozart's work from this point of view. Critics might nevertheless bear in mind that it is just this side of his work which has always been most admired by competent and professional judges. Surely it was just the songs which gave so much pleasure in his operas and other vocal compositions! Ordinary people understand little about the beauty of instrumentation. Just this part

[19]The author obtained this information direct from a famous German composer of operas, Herr P. von W[inter] who lived in Italy for some time, and who knows the state of music there, as he himself wrote several big operas for the stage.

of his work, which demands the greatest skill from
the players, is generally badly performed—and yet
his vocal compositions have such an effect and produce such enthusiasm. This could have been
achieved only by simple, beautiful, rhythmical
song. Why is one still so happy to sing his melodies?
Why have so many of them become popular songs?
How accurately and in what a lively manner
Mozart expresses the meaning of the poet's words!
Does not his song penetrate the listener's very heart?
If this is the ultimate aim of music, who, indeed,
has attained it more successfully than Mozart?

We could cite many examples in which Mozart,
with his fine aesthetic feelings, has enhanced and
improved the words and ideas of the poet by the
subtlety of his melody. It is generally only through
his songs that warmth and life are breathed into
them; nearly always he has supplied them with more
warmth and feeling than the actual words possessed.
That is why quite indifferent poems have found
favour, merely through his music. *The Magic Flute*
and *Cosi fan Tutti* are evidence of this. Which composer can compare with Mozart in his compositions
for many voices, finales and choruses?

'But Mozart's works are so difficult, so critical,
so full of art, but so little for the ear.' In like manner
school-boys often complain about the obscurity and
difficulties of Horace. One cannot help smiling.
Who is to blame? Did Mozart merely write for
students? Or is what he wrote for them not easy
and comprehensible? The difficulties in his works
are not intentional, but are merely the consequences
of his greatness and the originality of his genius.
This Mozart has in common with all great artists.

Not every work was intended to be popular. Where popularity was called for he achieved it successfully. In his comic operas, does not the expert, as well as the mere music-lover, find something to suit his palate? Even the noblest works flowing from his pen, in which he shows his great mastery of counterpoint, have so much intrinsic beauty that they please the most untrained ear, when they are played correctly and in a fitting manner! But there is the snag! For that is mostly the reason for such complaints. Above all, his music demands pure feeling and an unspoilt ear. Mozart did not write for those who do not possess these attributes.

The criticism of a class of people whom his music displeases does not weigh against his excellence. Similarly, Raphael's fame is not lessened because a gay trifle painted by a dabbler catches the eye of a lordly tailor's apprentice more readily than Raphael's masterpieces. Or have there never been people who have found the uncouth pipes of Pan more to their liking than the heavenly notes of Apollo? Those who find Mozart's music wanting, really should look for the fault in themselves. What would such delicate ears make of some of our younger composers?

Absolute havoc is now being wrought with his works by adapters and publishers who are imposing on the public and by whom the reputation of the great master is being much debased. He is saddled with many spurious works quite unworthy of his genius, and what is worse, often incompetent adapters patch together piano pieces from his larger works, and sell them as though they were originals, which are obviously not in the same class as his genuine piano compositions.

It is equally unfortunate that through lack of new works from his masterly hand, older compositions, partly written in his youth, are published without the fact being disclosed to the public. These works are frequently quite unlike his later ones, and cannot possess the same stamp of perfection.

Would not music-lovers like to have a correct and authentic edition of his best works compiled from the original scores in the possession of his widow?

To get a better conspectus, his works may be divided into eleven different categories. In the *first* we reckon the dramatic works: Mozart wrote nine Italian operas, three German ones:—

Italian Operas

La finta semplice, opera buffa for Emperor Joseph,
(1768)
Mitridate, opera seria for Milan,   (1770)
Lucio Silla,   (1772)
La finta Giardiniera, opera buffa for Emperor Joseph,
(1774)
Idomeneo, opera seria,   (1780)
Le Nozze di Figaro, opera buffa for Vienna, (1786)
Don Giovanni, opera buffa for Prague,   (1787)
Cosi fan tutte, opera buffa for Vienna,   (1790)
La Clemenza di Tito, opera seria, for Prague, (1791)

German Operas

Die Entführung aus dem Serail, for Vienna,   (1782)
Der Schauspieldirektor, an operetta for Emperor Joseph in Schoenbrunn,   (1786)
Die Zauberflöte for Schikaneder's Theatre,   (1791)
Idomeneo is one of his greatest works and richest in

thought; the style is in a sad vein and breathes heroic splendour throughout. As he wrote this opera for great singers and for one of the best orchestras in Europe, his spirit felt no restraint and could unfold luxuriously. But *Idomeneo* must be performed better than it was at Prague a few summers ago, when the opera producer missed its meaning altogether. It was indeed a peculiar idea to perform one of the greatest operas without good singers or orchestra, for both were lacking and were replaced by substitutes. We should also beware of judging this opera, or any other Mozart operas, by mediocre piano arrangements![20]

Figaro ranks highest amongst connoisseurs; it is true that Mozart worked hardest at its composition. In wealth of ideas it is equal to *Idomeneo*; as regards originality it is second to none.

Don Giovanni is recognised as the greatest masterpiece—great art and infinite charm are happily united.

Cosi fan tutte or *The School for Lovers* has delightful and playful music full of character and expression.

La Clemenza di Tito is considered from an aesthetic standpoint a fine work of art and is thought to be the most polished. With his fine sensitivity, Mozart comprehended the simplicity, the quiet nobility of the character of Titus and the whole plot, and conveyed this throughout his composition. Every part, even the smallest instrumental part, bears this stamp, and combines to form a beautifully united whole. As it was written for a coronation and for

[20]Even today while I am writing, it is again being performed by the Guardason Company, to full houses, after ten years —this winter already for the tenth time.

two singers specially engaged from Italy, he was
compelled to write brilliant arias for these two roles.
But what arias these were! Far above the usual
showy songs. The remaining scenes all proclaim
the great genius whence they flowed. The last scene
or Finale of the first Act is certainly the most
perfect of Mozart's work; expression, character,
feeling, all compete with one another to produce the
greatest effect. The singing, instrumentation,
variety of tone and echo of distant choruses—at
each performance these create such an impression
and illusion as is seldom apparent at operas. Among
all the choruses I have heard, there is none which is
so flowing, so noble, and so full of expression as the
final chorus of Act II; among all the arias, none so
charming, so filled with sweet melancholy, with
such a wealth of musical beauty as the complete
Rondo in F, with the Basset-horn obligato, 'Non
piu di Fiori' in Act II. The recitative with slight
instrumentation is by Mozart; the rest—much to
be regretted—is all in a pupil's hand.

The opera, which is still heard with delight, was
not liked as much as it deserved to be at its first
performance at the Coronation. A public which was
surfeited with dances, balls and amusements, in the
bustle of coronation festivities, certainly did not
find the simple beauties of Mozart's art much to its
taste!

Among the German comic operas, *Die Entführung*
is notable for its feeling and the beauty of song.
It is obvious that it was written soon after *Idomeneo*.

The little operetta *The Impresario* was merely
commissioned for a special performance at the Imperial Court at Schoenbrunn. What can I say about

Die Zauberflöte? Who in Germany does not know it? Is there a single theatre where it has not been performed? It is our national opera. The applause which it has received everywhere from the Court Theatre to the travelling players in the smallest market place is unparalleled. In Vienna, in the first year of its appearance, it was performed more than a hundred times.

In Prague it was first performed for two years in German, then in Italian, finally even in Bohemian, and it is still performed in this language on Sundays at the New Theatre.[21]

Mozart left an unfinished Italian opera.

The *second class* of his works includes compositions for the piano. Here the piano concertos are foremost, whose greatness and unsurpassable beauty have enhanced his fame considerably. And yet he is supposed to have written these unwillingly!

The sonatas with and without accompaniment are in everybody's hands. Among them the trios are the most original. The famous quintet for piano with accompaniment for oboe, clarinet, horn and bassoon is considered by connoisseurs as his masterpiece as regards instrumentation. It was written on 30 March 1784.

The many variations—through their riches, virtuosity and novelty—are distinguishable from all similar works. The last variations which he composed on 15 March 1791 were on the theme 'Ein Weib ist das herrlichste Ding'. He was most prolific in this type of composition.

[21]The continued pleasure given by Mozart's works in Prague is all the more remarkable, as musical taste has been visibly deteriorating in the last few years, owing to the bad productions which are being sent over by Vienna.

The *third class* consists of symphonies, the most beautiful of which, written between 1786 and 1788, are the following four: in D, E flat, G minor, and C, with the Fugue to the last-named. All of these can be compared with the best of Haydn. He unfolded his art of composition in them in a perfect manner. The opera overtures are well-known and have been admired sufficiently.

The cantatas for special occasions with choral accompaniment belong to the *fourth class*. In his catalogue three are mentioned.

In the *fifth class* we may group single scenes and arias which he wrote for musical 'Accademias' or for special singers. The catalogue enumerates twenty-two of these for various voices.

The *sixth class* comprises German songs with piano accompaniment only. In the catalogue twenty items are listed, among which are the famous 'Abendempfindung', 'Das Veilchen' and 'An Chloe' —so simple, so full of feeling and expression, in short so beautiful, that Mozart could certainly have achieved immortal fame with these alone. Here are excellent examples for critics to judge whether he was not a great composer of songs—whether he did not understand how to give life to words, even without the murmur of instruments.

Seventh class. He very seldom wrote concerti for different instruments. In his catalogue only the following are mentioned:

(1) Andante for a violin concerto
(2) Concerto for horn
(3) For the harmonica
(4) For the clarinet.

Eighth class. Violin quartets and quintets. The

six quartets dedicated to Joseph Haydn are the most beautiful; later in the year 1789—in June— he wrote three concertante quartets for the late King of Prussia; besides these there is a single quartet in D, written in 1786, and a single fugue.

There are only four original quintets enumerated in the catalogue; in C, G minor, D Major and E flat. He also wrote some serenades with accompaniment of two horns, which can be counted as violin concerti—all these works are filled with beautiful ideas. A concertante divertimento is for three parts, violin, viola and 'cello, and is unbelievably beautiful and of great artistic merit.

The two duets for violin and viola are well known and much admired.

Ninth class. Partitas for wind instruments for table and night music. Here in Prague much of this is well-known. Their beauty is enchanting, and moves the most insensitive heart. There is also in existence a serenade for thirteen wind instruments written by him.

Tenth class. Dance music. Mozart wrote several pieces, minuets and German dances for the Imperial Ballroom in Vienna. How much his work was sought can be seen from his catalogue, as many minuets, German dances, waltzes and 'contra-dances' were composed for the many court Carnivals.

Eleventh class. Church music. This was Mozart's favourite form of composition. But he was able to dedicate himself least of all to it. The Masses which he has left were composed for various occasions, and were specially commissioned. All those we have heard in Prague bear the stamp of his genius. In the catalogue no single Mass is mentioned, a proof that all those that we have, must be placed in the early years of his life. He, however, composed a gradual on the text 'Ave verum corpus' in June 1791. Here in Prague some motets have been made, based on his compositions, which are sung by various church choirs with dignity and solemnity.

Mozart could have shown his full powers in this branch of music only if he had, in fact, obtained the post at St Stephen's Church; he looked forward to it. How well his gifts could have been used for this type of serious church music is proved by his last work, the Requiem Mass, which certainly surpasses anything that has previously been achieved in this sphere.

Apart from these categories of his work, he also left ten canons for voice only, i.e. eight for four-part and two for three-part songs, some serious, others humorous. They are not only masterpieces, but also very entertaining.

In conclusion, we must narrate an incident which tells us more than a laudatory speech. An old Italian impresario of an opera company in Germany, who seems to have fallen on evil days ever since the rise of Mozart, as no opera, least of all those written by foreign composers, has met with any success, is wont to heave a sigh whenever he comes across an opera of Mozart's in his list, and to utter the cry: 'He is my undoing'.

The author has made use of the following sources
in the writing of this book:

(1) His own experience and his intercourse with
Mozart's family and friends.

(2) The witness of many trustworthy people,
whom Mozart knew at various periods of
his life.

(3) Information, papers and letters supplied by
his surviving widow, for whose friendly help
I am most grateful.

(4) With regard to Mozart's youth, Schlichtegroll's *Nekrolog* has been of much assistance.

The author has tried to be scrupulously honest
and has left out many an interesting occurrence if its
veracity seemed at all doubtful.